BETTER WINEMAKING & BREWING FOR BEGINNERS

By the same author

IMPROVE YOUR WINEMAKING

AB-Z OF WINEMAKING

(in conjunction with E. A. Roycroft)

BETTER WINEMAKING & BREWING FOR BEGINNERS

B. C. A. Turner

PELHAM BOOKS

First published in Great Britain by
PELHAM BOOKS LTD
52 *Bedford Square*
*London, W.C.*1
OCTOBER 1971
SECOND IMPRESSION SEPTEMBER 1972

© 1971 *by B. C. A. Turner*

7207 0518 5

*Printed in Great Britain by
Hollen Street Press Ltd at Slough
and bound by James Burn at Esher, Surrey*

For my beloved wife
whose love sustains me
when my muse deserts me

CONTENTS

ILLUSTRATIONS

Plates 1–6 are of equipment kindly loaned by W. R. Loftus Ltd and plates 7, 8, 9 and 10 are reproduced by courtesy of *Good Housekeeping*

CHAPTER ONE

Introduction

At first glance the contents of this book may appear to be in the wrong order. In other books you may have seen on this subject the theory is often at the front of the book and the recipes are usually set out at the back. There is much to be said for such a plan. It is logical, progressive and orthodox. But the best way to learn is by doing. In this book, then, four recipes that make superb wines come first and in great detail, so that if you have the equipment and ingredients readily available, you can start off straight away to make excellent wine. You can learn the theory as you go along. Recipes for all occasions are given later on.

The theory is very important, however, especially in the fermentation of the must into the new wine. You are strongly recommended to read chapter 6 very carefully so that you can fully understand how the sugar is turned into alcohol and the bubbles of gas called carbon dioxide. A proper appreciation of the principles of fermentation, will, for example, enable you to produce really dry table wines without difficulty. This knowledge will also enable you to control accurately the alcohol content of your wines and beers. To be able to do so is most important because a good wine is one that is well balanced for its kind. A red table wine for example needs to be dry, vinous, of moderate acidity, have a taste of tannin and contain between 10 per cent and 12 per cent alcohol by volume. If the alcohol has been allowed to reach 15 per cent because the principles of fermentation have not been understood, then the wine will be unbalanced and far too strong for its purpose as a table wine. Such a wine should be sweetened and served in smaller quantities as a dessert wine.

It should be thoroughly well appreciated right from the start, that the purpose of making wine and beer at home is to produce good sound beverages for every day enjoyment. It is NOT to make wine and beer so strong that a few glasses make you drunk. Mostly wine should be served with food, whether it is a full meal, cheese and biscuits, shortbread or fruit cake.

The same wine tastes differently when served with different food. A dry red table wine for example, may taste superb when served with roast beef, Yorkshire pudding, roast potatoes and cauliflower. But when drunk with sweet apple pie and cream, it will taste sour, harsh and quite unpleasant. The same remark is true of commercial wines, of course, and does not apply only to home made wines.

Each wine has its own purpose and tastes better when properly served with appropriate food. (See chapter 10.) The great advantage of making wine at home is that you can make a good supply of different wines for different purposes at a cost of no more than 5p a bottle and often much less. This will enable you to serve an appropriate wine with almost any meal and so enjoy both to their best advantage.

If you have never made wine before, you are recommended to read through at least once the chapters on Preparation, Fermentation and Maturation. This will give you a little background on which to tackle your first recipe where itemised instructions are given in chronological order. As you progress you can refer again and again to the theory until you need to do so no longer.

It is not possible to repeat every single minute detail under each recipe and sometimes a different action has to be taken in the light of the development of the wine. For example, if the fermentation ceases while there is still plenty of sugar in the must, steps must be taken to get it going again. This is fully set out on page 38, but it is unnecessary and tedious to repeat this for every recipe. This problem very rarely arises; most wine makers meet it only occasionally. Clearly, however, there must always be some information given in the theory that is not constantly repeated in the recipes.

The recipes given in the book have all been carefully designed and tested in the light of the latest technical knowledge and long experience, to give excellent results. Once in a blue moon however, something doesn't go quite according to plan, and then you need to know just what to do to put matters right. This is all set out in the text and is mentioned here only to encourage you to read it. Furthermore, palates vary, and a little knowledge of the theory does help enormously in modifying the recipes to suit your particular taste. It should be remembered also that there can frequently be wide variations in the quality of the fruit available to you. These variations occur not only between one part of the country and another but between one year and another. A year of splendid sunshine such as 1970 yielded a crop of sweet fruit of good flavour. A cold wet summer, however, can yield fruit that is high in acidity and poor in flavour. The same recipe using the same fruits will obviously produce different wines from year to year, just as the commercial wines vary.

Happily the variations in the quality of fruit is often more subtle than dramatic and, by and large, the recipes given will yield wines of high average quality. During the 1960s scientists developed a technique known as gas chromatography. In simple terms, gases or liquids can be analysed in such a way that even very small quantities of volatile substances can be detected.

Applied to winemaking this means that the substances that cause 'off' flavours can be sorted out from those that cause pleasant and enjoyable sensations.

Whilst applied analysis is still going on by a few research scientists, we already know for certain, that which a handful of winemakers including the author, long suspected. As far back as 1952 the author became aware of the benefits accruing from blending wines and fruits and has constantly urged other winemakers to blend their less successful wines and to use multiple ingredients in the preparation of a must.

Now we have scientific evidence that the blending encourages the development of pleasing odours and flavours and mitigates those that are unwelcome.

During fermentation certain of the original odours and flavours diminish while others are created by the activities of the actual yeast being used. This is why it is so important to use a good quality wine yeast suitable for the must and the kind of wine you wish to make.

The benefits of the right proportion of free sulphur dioxide, in white wines in particular, are now being more appreciated. Campden tablets, sometimes known as metabisulphite either of potassium or sodium, have long been used by some winemakers and shunned by others who fear that they may end up with a sulphury taste in their wine. A newer anti-microbial substance is now being tested. It is called diethyl-pyrocarbonate or DEPC for short. Its great advantage is that it is not only more effective in suppressing unwanted bacteria and fungi but eventually decomposes into natural elements already in wine.

The need to use a pectin destroying enzyme to obtain the utmost flavour from the ingredients and to ensure a good wine are now widely known.

The recipes in this book take these latest scientific developments into account and not only enable you to produce excellent 'vin ordinaire' every time, but also provide the basis for the not infrequent really superb wine, depending of course on the quality and suitability of the fruit and other ingredients.

More than twenty-five years study and experience has taught the author that whilst you can make wine from the most unlikely ingredients such as peapods and even birch sap, nevertheless fruit consistently makes better wine than other ingredients. Most of the recipes given in this book then have a fruit base. These are not gimmicky wines but 'do you good' wines made for drinking as an accompaniment to food.

CHAPTER TWO

Some step-by-step recipes to start you off

SUMMER FRUIT WINE

To be made in July every year.

Ingredients
½ lb blackcurrants
½ lb redcurrants
½ lb whitecurrants (if available)
½ lb raspberries
½ lb gooseberries
1 lb rhubarb/plums/grapes/or other similar fruit
6 oz chopped raisins or sultanas
6 oz white honey if available
1½–2 lb white granulated sugar depending on the sweetness of the fruit
3 qts of cold water or enough to make the finished must up to 9 pints (about 5 litres)
1 teaspoonful of Pectolase or Pectinol, 2 Campden tables
Champagne or Burgundy yeast

Method
1 Wash and prepare the fruit, i.e. remove stalks, stones, tops and tails, and rinse in clean cold water to remove dust and dirt.
2 Place the fruit in a clean mashing vessel after you have crushed the berries, chopped the rhubarb and raisins etc.
3 Add one crushed Campden tablet and a teaspoonful of Pectinol. Then pour on the cold water – 3 qts in the first instance.
4 Cover the vessel closely and leave it for 24 hours.
5 Remove the cover and squeeze the fruit in your hands so as to ensure that it is thoroughly broken up.

6 Strain some of the liquid into a trial jar and check the specific gravity with your hydrometer, making a note of the reading.

7 Return the contents of the trial jar to the mashing vessel. Add a crushed nutrient tablet and an active yeast, and finally replace the cover of the vessel.

8 On each of the next 5 days remove the cover, stir the must well – pressing down into the liquid the fruit pulp supported on the surface by the rising gas – and replace the cover.

9 Strain the juice through a linen cloth and press the fruit pulp dry with your hands.

10 Stir in and thoroughly dissolve the honey and enough sugar to bring the specific gravity to 1.085.

(First deduct from 85 the number you noted when first checking the must under 6 above, then deduct 9 for the honey, divide the result by 2 and this is the number of ounces of sugar that you need to bring the specific gravity up to 1.085.)

Assume that the first reading was 12. Deduct from 85 and you have 73, take away a further 9 for the honey and you are left with 64, divide by 2 and you have 32, which is the number of ounces of sugar to add i.e. 2 lb.

11 Measure the quantity of must that you have and if needs be add some cold boiled water to bring it up to 9 pints.

12 Pour the fermenting must into fermentation jar and fit an airlock.

13 Surplus must should be placed in a bottle, plugged with cotton-wool and stood beside the jar.

14 Affix to the jar an appropriate label on which is set out the ingredients and the date fermentation started and stand the jar and bottle in a warm place, i.e. 65°–70°F.

15 When fermentation is finished and the wine begins to clear, check the specific gravity again. It should now read 1.000 or thereabouts, possibly a little lower.

16 Rack the new wine with the aid of a siphon into a clean storage jar and add another crushed Campden tablet and top up with the surplus wine.

17 Bung the jar tight, label it and store it in a cool dark place for 2 months.

18 Carefully bring the jar out of storage and siphon the now bright wine from its sediment into another clean storage jar. Fill up the jar with wine or a little cold boiled water.

19 Replace the bung and label and return the jar to store for a further 3 months.

20 Examine the jar again and if there is the least trace of sediment, as there will most likely be, siphon the clean wine into another storage jar. Bung and label the jar and return it to store until the following April.

21 Round about Easter rack the finished wine into six clean wine bottles that have been rinsed with a solution of 1 Campden tablet dissolved in ½ pint of cold water.

22 Cork the bottles with clean cylindrical corks that have been soaked for 24 hours in a similar Campden tablet solution.

23 Label and store the bottles on their sides for a further few months.

Not earlier than the date on which you started the wine in the previous year, try a bottle of the wine. It should be nicely chilled and served with roast lamb, new potatoes and garden peas. The wine should be a deep pink or a light red and medium dry to dry depending on whether you used Champagne yeast or Burgundy yeast (dry). It should have a fresh and full bouquet and taste clean, fruity, smooth and well-balanced. It will contain about 11 per cent alcohol. It will keep for several years but will not improve much more.

AUTUMN HARVEST – A dry table wine

Ingredients
1 lb blackberries
½ lb fresh elderberries and/or ½ lb fresh sloes
2 lb red cooking plums
4–6 lb apples and/or pears preferably of the cooking variety
2 lb grapes or 8 oz grape juice concentrate or 8 oz sultanas
4–4½ lb sugar
6 quarts water
1 oz acid (citric or tartaric)
2 teaspoonfuls of Pectolase
2 Campden tablets
1 nutrient tablet
Burgundy or Pommard yeast

Method

1 Prepare the fruit by removing stalks, leaves, stones and any bruised portions.

2 Wash it in a bowl of water to which has been added 1 crushed Campden table and a little citric acid.

3 Drain the fruit and crush it well, especially the apples and pears, place it in a mashing vessel already containing the 6 quarts of water, 1 teaspoonful of Pectolase, 1 nutrient tablet, 1 Campden tablet and the acid, cover and leave for 24 hours.

4 Stir in an active yeast, cover the vessel closely and stand in a warm position.

5 Next day stir the must thoroughly and strain out enough liquid to test the specific gravity. Record the reading.

6 Ferment on the pulp for 5 or 6 days, then strain off all the solids and press the pulp as dry as you can.

7 Stir in sufficient sugar to increase the specific gravity to 1.080 (deduct your first hydrometer reading from 1.080 and add 2 lb sugar for each 32 units. E.g. natural specific gravity of must 1.016, take from 1.080 leaves 0.064, so add a total of 4 lb sugar).

8 Pour the must into a fermentation vessel, fit an air lock and leave to ferment to dryness.

9 As soon as the wine starts to clear, rack it from its lees, add 1 crushed Campden tablet per gallon.

10 Store in the dark and cool until a further deposit appears, then rack again, add another Campden tablet and return to store.

11 After 10 months bottle and store for a further 6 to 8 months before serving free from chill.

Note

This dry table wine is excellent with all roasted red meats, turkey and so on. It is first class with cheese and biscuits served at the end of the day.

A sweet version of this wine may be made by increasing the total fruit content by 2 lb and by using an additional 1 lb sugar. In these circumstances it is preferable to use a port wine yeast. After the first 8 steps mentioned above the further 1 lb sugar should be stirred in the fermentation continued. If needs be a further ½ lb sugar should be stirred in when the specific gravity has fallen again to 1.000.

The final specific gravity should read about 1.015.

The wine is then finished in the way set out above but this sweeter version will need a little longer storing to achieve its best result. It should be served as a dessert wine at the end of a meal, preferably with the cheese.

WINTER DELIGHT

Ingredients
8 Seville oranges
2 lb cooking apples
4 oz figs
8 oz white grape juice concentrate
3 lb sugar
1 gallon water
Sauterne yeast
1 teaspoonful Pectolase
1 nutrient tablet
Campden tablets

Method
1 Wipe the oranges clean and thinly pare only 4 of them. Exclude the bitter white pith.
2 Cut all the oranges in halves and squeeze out all the juice.
3 Put the juice and rinds into a mashing vessel together with 1 gallon of cold water, 1 crushed Campden tablet and 1 teaspoonful of Pectolase.
4 Wash the apples, crush them into small pieces and drop them into the water without delay.
5 Wash the figs, break them into pieces and add them to the apples.
6 Cover the vessel and leave it in the warm for 24 hours.
7 Next day stir in the grape juice concentrate, 1 lb sugar, the crushed nutrient tablet and an active yeast.
8 Cover the vessel and ferment in a warm place for 6 or 7 days.
9 Strain the must off the pulp and stir in the remaining sugar.
10 Pour the wine into a fermentation jar, fit an air lock and continue the fermentation at 70°F.
11 When fermentation slows down and the specific gravity has dropped to 1.010 or just below, rack into a clean jar and add 2 crushed Campden tablets. Replace the air lock.

12 When the wine clears, rack into a clean storage jar, add 1 more crushed Campden tablet and store for 6–9 months.

13 Bottle and store for another 6 months. Serve cold.

SPRING VINTAGE

Ingredients

3 lb fresh rhubarb
½ lb dried apricots
½ lb bananas
8 oz white grape juice concentrate. Rind only of 1 large lemon
2¾ lb sugar
1 gallon water
Sherry yeast
1 teaspoonful Pectolase
1 nutrient tablet
Campden tablets

Method

1 Top and tail the rhubarb, wipe the stalks with a clean damp cloth, cut them into small pieces and place them in a mashing vessel.

2 Wash the dried apricots, peel the bananas cut them into pieces and add them to the rhubarb.

3 Thinly pare a lemon and add the rind to the fruit avoid the white pith which is very bitter.

4 Pour one gallon of boiling water on to the fruit and cover the vessel closely.

5 When cool add 1 teaspoonful of Pectolase and 1 crushed Campden tablet, re-cover the vessel and leave it in a warm place for 24 hours.

6 Stir in the white grape juice concentrate, ¾ lb sugar and then 1 crushed nutrient tablet and active Sherry yeast.

7 Again cover the vessel and leave for 5 days, but stir twice each day to keep the floating fruit wet.

8 Strain off the fruit and stir in the rest of the sugar, taking care to avoid wastage caused by foaming.

9 Pour the must into a fermentation jar, fit an air lock and leave in a warm place (70°F).

10 When fermentation is finished and the wine begins to clear rack the new wine into a storage jar and add another crushed Campden tablet.

11 As soon as the wine is clear, rack again into a clean storage jar and keep for 6–12 months.

12 Bottle and store for a further 3 months.

13 Serve cold (55°F.) with light meals.

CHAPTER THREE

Basic Equipment

Although the basic equipment for making wine is quite simple, there are many aids that have been developed in recent years. The more useful will be mentioned, although not every single item is essential.

Many of the items serve a dual use in the kitchen and in the winery and if the quantity of wine that you propose to make is small it is not worthwhile getting separate pieces. If, however, you intend to go into winemaking in a big way, say about 50 gallons a year, then it is worthwhile having your own pieces reserved solely for winemaking.

The first item required is a vessel in which to mash the wine, i.e. to extract all the goodness, flavour, sugar, acid, tannin and many minor substances from the fruit or other base ingredients. The most popular vessel in use today is a 4-gallon plastic dustbin-like tub with a close fitting lid. It costs about 75p and can be obtained in many shops in every High Street. A larger version holding about 15 gallons is also available, and essential if you are making substantial quantities of apple wine, for example.

A wooden tub or cask with one end removed and the bung hole filled-in is quite effective but it is very heavy and much more difficult to keep clean than the plastic container already mentioned.

There are still some earthenware pots about, glazed on the inside. They are available in various sizes and excellent for the purpose. They are, however, somewhat heavy. It is wise never to use ancient crocks of this kind which may have been lined with a lead glaze rather than the salt glaze used in more recent years. The acid in the wine combines with the lead in the glaze to form a poisonous substance. For this reason metal containers of all kinds should be avoided like the plague. This does not exclude boiling pans, however, which are used solely for boiling vegetables without acid, or for bringing a honey solution to the boil to sterilize it and extract the dirty waxes and scum. Must containing acid and wine which also contains acid, of course, should never be left in any metal container, nor should it come into contact with anything metal in the way of utensils.

There is no doubt that a good quality plastic bucket or tub is infinitely superior to anything previously available. It is cheap, light, easy to clean, easy to dry, inert to acids and alkalis and easy to graduate for quantities if it is so desired.

FRUIT CRUSHER

A pestle is a great aid in crushing soft fruit but the end of a rolling pin or a baulk of wood, say 4 in. square and 10 in. long attached to a broom handle does equally well. It is especially helpful when crushing hard fruit such as apples.

A big wooden spoon is essential for stirring must and if possible should be kept for this purpose.

STRAINER

When all the goodness has been extracted from the fruit the juice has to be strained, and a large nylon sieve is extremely useful for this purpose. At one time butter muslin was used. This is not very robust and a linen sack or pillowcase is much stronger and easier to use.

There are now many small and reasonably priced presses on the market and any serious winemaker should certainly possess one. It takes a tremendous amount of hard work out of this process especially if a substantial quantity of wine is being made at one time. The handyman can fairly easily make a suitable press for his own use but it needs to be made extremely strong and no metal should be used in its construction where it is likely to come into contact with the acid fruit juice. All the wood should be thoroughly coated several times with polyurethane to facilitate cleaning.

Liquidisers and juice extractors may of course be used. There is no particular saving in time since the juice from the liquidiser or extractor will still need to be sulphited for twenty-four hours before the yeast is added.

FERMENTATION VESSELS

Fermentation vessels are available in great variety, although the most popular is still the 1-gallon glass jar. Because it is transparent you can see what is going on inside the jar, how the wine is clearing, how much deposit has been thrown and so on. In a gallon size it is easy to handle and easy to clean. 5-gallon glass carboys are popular for larger quantities. Similar vessels are available in high density polythene.

Obviously a wooden cask can also be used, and one can even buy plastic bags with a narrow neck fitting which one can accommodate temporarily inside a cardboard box. Narrow neck earthenware jars are also in use. They have the advantage of keeping the temperature of the fermentation steady, but of course are heavy to handle.

The essential feature of any fermentation vessel is that the neck should be sufficiently narrow to contain a bung fitted with an air lock. The purpose of the air lock is of course to keep out the air containing bacteria, moulds and fungi as well as dust, and yet will release the carbon dioxide gushing up from the must. The most popular air locks are made from plastic but one can still buy glass locks. The lock is actually a few drops of sulphited water which you put into the plastic or glass container in such a way that the carbon dioxide can bubble through from the inside but the air cannot get in from the outside. A good pad of clean cotton wool can sometimes be used instead, since this enables the gas to percolate through it and acts as an adequate filter for any fungi or bacteria. Air locks are essential pieces of equipment. They cost very little and repay their cost time and time again.

The most valuable instrument which the serious winemaker must have is an hydrometer and trial jar. They cost no more than 50p each and are absolutely essential to the making of quality wine. By using the hydrometer regularly you can find out how much natural sugar is present in the juice or must and how much sugar you need to add to make a wine of a given alcoholic strength. Knowing how much sugar was present when fermentation started enables you to calculate the percentage of alcohol by volume in the finished wine. This is often indicated on the hydrometer itself. At the end of fermentation you can also tell by using the hydrometer whether the wine has fermented to dryness or whether residual sugar still remains. The instrument is simplicity itself to use, no more difficult than an ordinary thermometer. It can be used for beer and mead as well as wine and will greatly facilitate achieving a good brew as a regular standard.

An ordinary water thermometer is very useful to have about to ensure that the must is of a suitable temperature to receive an active yeast, and also when making a hot punch, to ensure that the temperature of the punch never exceeds 145°F.

SIPHON

A siphon is another essential piece of equipment. It can be as simple as 4 ft of rubber tubing, $\frac{1}{2}$ in in diameter, or it can be more sophisticated with a 'U' tube at one end, or alternatively a blocked end with a few holes above it and a pump on the other end to save you sucking the wine through the tube. A laboratory clip is available to use instead of your fingers when you wish to close the siphon. Since every wine has to be racked three or four times before being bottled, the siphon is going to be in great use – perhaps even daily use. Racking is the name given to the process of siphoning the clear wine from a jar containing sediment into another jar in such a way as to leave the sediment behind. In wine and beer making racking and siphoning are synonymous. A variety of sizes of plastic funnels are also of considerable use and from time to time you are sure to want to use each of several different sizes.

Vessels in which wine has been fermented may also be used for storage and it is sufficient to replace the air lock with a solid cork or rubber bung of good quality. Clear glass storage jars should be covered in brown paper to keep out the light during maturation. Casks must be rested in a cradle on their sides and are best stored on a shelf to facilitate racking and bottling. Earthenware jars are often best for storage, however, since they are easy to clean, maintain a stable temperature and keep out the light.

At the time of writing there has has not been sufficient time to evaluate experiments using plastic containers for maturation purposes. They are certainly all right for short periods provided they are absolutely clean and absolutely free from odour of any kind. They are usually fitted with poor fitting screw caps however, and there is a tendency for wine to evaporate from them. Plastic barrels are available for the beer maker and these can be stored on their end. Frequently a tap is fitted at the bottom so that the beer can be drawn off and sometimes the equivalent of a soda siphon sparklet is fitted so that the beer can be carbonated as and when required.

BOTTLES

Wine bottles are essential for bottling wine. Beer bottles are essential for bottling beer and Champagne bottles are essential for bottling sparkling wine. This is not to conform with fashion but rather to provide a bottle sufficiently strong for the purpose for which it is to be used. Spirit bottles, orange and squash bottles are far too fragile to be risked in case the pressure builds up within the wine, especially in hot weather. Beer has to have a secondary fermentation in the bottle to produce the necessary carbon dioxide to give it life and vitality when poured. This pressure is considerable and on no account should any other type of bottle be used for beer. The same rule applies to sparkling wines. Pressure of up to 90 lb per square inch can build up in the wine during its secondary fermentation, and it is absolutely essential for the thickness of the glass to be increased to withstand this strain.

CORKS

Cylindrical or flanged corks may be used for storing wine. If the wine is likely to be in bottle for any length of time there is no doubt that a cylindrical cork should be used, but if it is purely a temporary matter a flange cork may be used. The latter can be easily used, washed, dried and used again, whilst the cylindrical cork has to be bored with a corkscrew to open the bottle and then becomes useless. Plastic corks are available but are not yet very popular since the neck size of bottles vary and the plastic stopper has little 'give' in it. Screw stoppers may be used with a beer bottle providing fresh rubber rings are used from time to time as the old ones soil and deteriorate. Alternatively, crown cork stoppers may now be used easily and readily as a hand crown corking machine has been perfected and is readily available on the market, costing only a few shillings. Champagne bottles need extra strong and good quality corks and these must be wired down.

Plastic or foil capsules are cheaply available in a variety of colours to cover the necks of bottles, including the top of the cork, and these give a professional finish to the appearance of a wine.

Alternatively the top of the cork may be waxed and this discourages the growth of mould.

CORKER

A hand corking gun has been available for some time and most inexpensively. It consists of a cylinder with a hole in the side in which the soft cork is placed when the piston is withdrawn. The wooden cylinder is then placed over the bottle, the piston pushed down, and in so doing squeezes the cork through a narrow entrance, the size of the neck of the bottle, and well down flush with the top. It is simplicity itself to use and needs only hand pressure. A piece of plastic covered wire is always worth keeping handy to slip into the neck of the bottle at the same time so that it can be withdrawn after the cork has been rammed home, thus releasing a small quantity of air and diminishing the pressure between the wine and the cork.

A bottle brush is essential for cleaning bottles and joins. It need cost only a few pence and will last a very long time.

Attractive self-adhesive wine labels in various designs and colours can be bought for little more than coppers.

If your house is sometimes rather cold a small heater and thermostat is worth buying to enable you to maintain your fermentation at a standard temperature. Some winemakers have built small cupboards for this purpose. They are called fermentation cupboards, are insulated and the temperature within is maintained at the ideal temperature for fermenting wine.

CHAPTER FOUR

Essential ingredients to keep by you

Good quality fresh fruit has advantages of flavour and bouquet over dried and canned fruits but the disadvantage with fresh fruit is that the wine has to be made at the time convenient to the fruit rather than to the winemaker since the fruit will otherwise deteriorate rapidly. Many winemaking suppliers now stock a large variety of canned and drier fruits as well as concentrates and syrups. Elderberries, bilberries, sloes, raisins, bananas, apricots, figs, rosehip shells, prunes and so on are nearly alway available. Honey from different parts of the world as far away as China and Mexico in the east and west, and Australia and New Zealand in the south, and Canada in the north can also be obtained. Everyone acknowledges, however, that English honey is the best.

Concentrated grape juice is also readily available, often imported from Spain and France. The gravity is usually about 1.385. A gallon is sufficient to make 4 to $4\frac{1}{2}$ gallons of wine, depending on the strength required. A quart of concentrate added to a 4-gallon must makes a tremendous improvement and increases the specific gravity of that must by about 20 units, so less sugar is required. The concentrate is usually available in quart, half gallon and gallon containers.

Recently available are some concentrated fruit compounds in a variety of different ingredients. The makers claim that it is sufficient to add $2\frac{1}{2}$ lb sugar and enough water to make up to 1 gallon, to add yeast and then to ferment the must into wine in the usual way. There has not yet been time to see how all these wines mature and it might well be that here again these concentrates are best used as additives to other fresh fruits to ensure a good blend of basic ingredients from which to start off your fermentation.

Every serious winemaker will want to keep in stock some citric acid and/or tartaric and malic acids. Some nutrient in the form of di-ammonium phosphate crystals or in tablet form, some sodium metabisulphite in powder form or in the form of Campden tablets, some Pectolase or Pectinol or other pectin destroying enzyme, some grape tannin powder or liquid and possibly some Bentonite for use in clearing cloudy wines.

A selection of different kinds of yeast should also be kept in stock as well as some raisins and sultanas.

There is nearly always some sugar available in every household. Experience suggests, however, that it is always well worthwhile keeping a few 2 lb bags as a standby.

Frequently the opportunity to make wine arises unexpectedly and it is most annoying not to have readily available some essential ingredient, so always keep some stock by you.

CHAPTER FIVE

Preparation of the must

Before reading this chapter it is probable that you have already made some wine. You may very well think then that it is not necessary to read any more on the subject of preparing the must for fermentation. If you do take the trouble to read these pages however, you should be able to find some information that is completely new to you or that will help you when you are making your next brew of wine.

There is no doubt that from time to time you will have access to certain fruits, flowers, roots, grains, tinned pulp and so on and you will be wondering whether it is suitable for you to use in making some wine. There is a tendency to try anything once, but if you are prepared to be guided by the mistakes of others you will confine yourself to well tested ingredients rather than to waste your efforts on unsuitable ingredients.

There is no doubt that the best wine is made from certain varieties of grape. Not all varieties are suitable for making wine and generally speaking those that are suitable for dessert purposes are not suitable for making wine. Many other fruits make very attractives wines, but here again it is usually the cooking varieties rather than the dessert varieties that are most suitable for wine-making. This applies particularly to apples and gooseberries. Very small quantities of dessert apples may be used in conjunction with cooking apples, crab apples, cider apples and so on, but used by themselves dessert apples make a very poor wine. Gooseberries are best for winemaking when they are still hard and green just before they ripen fully. Like raspberries dessert varieties of gooseberries have such a strong flavour that the wine tastes strongly of the fruit used. Very strongly flavoured fruits are always best when used in conjunction with other fruits. Eating varieties of cherries too are

30

quite useless for winemaking; without doubt the cooking varieties and the Morello variety are greatly superior. Pears are another example. Ripe dessert varieties are quite useless for winemaking although the cooking pear makes a superb white sparkling wine. Excellent wine has been made from carrots, parsnips and beetroot, but in making such wines great care must be taken to ensure that sufficient acid and tannin is added since the vegetables possess none of their own.

Delightfully scented and flavoured wine can be made from certain flowers but here again acid and tannin must be added together with some fruit pulp such as raisins or sultanas to ensure adequate fermentation and a balanced wine.

The flavour, goodness, sweetness, acidity, tannin etc., has to be extracted from the base ingredients. This can be done by crushing them and soaking them in water, by boiling them or by liquidising the fruit.

It is elementary, however, that before doing any of these things, the fruit, vegetables or grains should be washed clean and freed from any dust or dirt. Stalks must be removed where necessary and possible. Stones should be cut out. Hard fruit must be crushed but at the same time care should be taken to ensure that it does not oxidise in the process. For example apples may be crushed by placing a few clean apples at a time in a strong plastic or polythene bag and by hitting them with a mallet or some other piece of wood. As soon as the apples are crushed they should be dropped into water containing a dissolved Campden tablet to ensure that no browning or oxidisation takes place. This remark is true of all fruit. Wherever possible best quality fruit should be used but if this is not always possible, then the fruit should at least be free from any mould, bruised or damaged parts. These should be cut away and discarded otherwise they will taint the finished wine.

You will already have seen that the recipes recommend the use of Campden tablets. This is in effect potassium metabisulphite which is more commonly called sulphite. When dissolved in water the gas sulphur dioxide (SO_2) is given off and this inhibits the growth of moulds and fungi. Weak specimens are killed off and the stronger ones are prevented from developing. Happily it strengthens the best cells of the wine yeast and so its use in every recipe is strongly recommended. However, it is important to allow at least twenty-four hours to elapse between putting in sulphite in the form of a crushed Campden tablet or any equivalent solution and the adding of an active yeast. This is to ensure that the quantity of active sulphur dioxide is not so strong as to inhibit the growth and development of the added wine yeast.

The addition of a further crushed Campden tablet when putting the wine into store for the first time helps to stablise the wine and to prevent it from further fermentation in bottle or jar and to prevent oxidation. Sulphite also plays its part in clearing the finished wine by neutralising the negative charged colloids, thus causing them to settle rather than enabling them to combine with positively charged colloids.

If you are using the metabisulphite in powder form put $\frac{1}{4}$ oz powder in a wine bottle full of cold boiled water, cork it thoroughly and shake the bottle until the powder is dissolved. Half a fluid ounce of this solution, i.e. one dessertspoonful, is equivalent to 1 Campden tablet. For sterilising bottles, jars and all equipment, dissolve 6 Campden tablets and $\frac{1}{2}$ oz citric acid in 1 pint of cold boiled water, or $\frac{1}{4}$ oz of sodium or potassium metabisulphite powder and $\frac{3}{4}$ oz citric acid in one wine bottle full of cold boiled water. If stoppered tightly this solution can be used time and again during a bottling and cleaning session.

The use of sulphite is, therefore, most important. At least one Campden tablet per gallon should always be used during preparation, and if the fruit is not quite perfect than an extra tablet should be used.

Before you actually start to make a wine you should try to think of the kind of wine with which you hope to finish. Is it to be an apéritif wine, table wine, social wine or dessert wine for example? This will have an important bearing on the additional ingredients to be added at the time of preparation and the amount of sugar to be used as well. It is often a good idea to blend together a number of different fruits to help achieve a well balanced wine. Cereals and bananas either fresh or dried give body to a wine. Raisins or sultanas are always worth adding to give fruit mucilage and vinosity to the wine. More frequently nowadays grape juice concentrate is being used instead of the dried fruit and although this seems expensive in small quantities it does not add more than a few pence to the cost of each bottle of wine in say a 5-gallon brew.

Yeast is only active in a solution containing acid, and if there

Fruit crushers and presses. Well worth having

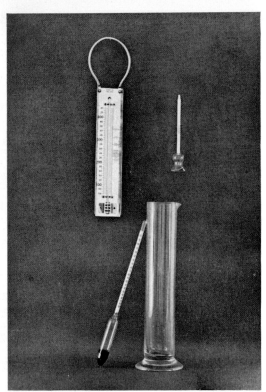

Thermometer, vinometer hanging up. Hydrometer with trial jar on the table. The latter is a most valuable aid to measuring the sugar content of liquids

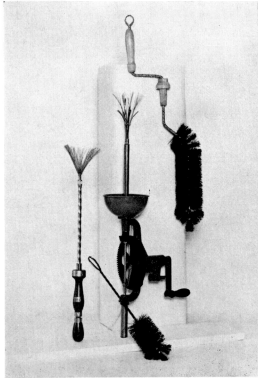

Assorted bottle and jar brushes. You need one of these

is any doubt as to whether the fruit contains sufficient acid, then citric acid crystals or the thinly pared rind and juice of lemons should be added. The wine will not ferment well without acid, and if insufficient is used the result is likely to taste like rather sweet medicine.

The same is true of tannin, which is found in fruit skins and stalks and especially in the skins and stalks of grapes. If the must is likely to be lacking in tannin, from $\frac{1}{8}$ to $\frac{1}{2}$ teaspoonful of grape tannin powder should be added to the must, or from $\frac{1}{3}$ to $\frac{1}{2}$ cup cold strong tea, which also contains a considerable quantity of tannin.

Nearly all fruit contains some pectin. This substance is found in the cell wall surrounding the tiny drops of juice and if these walls are not thoroughly broken down and dissolved they will float in the finished wine causing a haze. The problem can easily be solved by adding at this stage a pectin destroying enzyme such as Pectolase. This not only helps to achieve a clear wine but greatly helps in the extraction of all the goodness and flavour.

Yeast cells need nourishment in the form of nitrogen and this is usually readily available in fruit and vegetable musts. After dilution in water, however, the quantity is frequently insufficient and it is always advisable to add some di-ammonium phosphate as nutrient for the yeast. Half a teaspoonful per gallon is adequate but this substance can also be obtained in tablet form and it is sufficient to add one tablet per gallon. The merit of this additive is to ensure a good continuous fermentation without interruption and the attainment of a dry wine when fermentation is completed.

The final ingredient to add is the water and this can be either hot or cold. By pouring boiling water on to fruit it softens more readily and it is thought that a better extraction of the juice or flavour is obtained. Although it takes slightly longer, cold water will achieve the same result and without any risk of dissipating essential but volatile substances.

Fermentation on the pulp is becoming increasingly popular because it enables cold water to be used and an early start to fermentation, thus avoiding the risk of leaving a must lying around where it might pick up infection from moulds or fungi. Furthermore as the alcohol is formed during the process of fermentation, it assists in the further extraction of sweetness, flavour and goodness from the fruit. Fermentation on the pulp can be continued

C

too long, however, since when the fruit mucelage begins to decompose it can impart off-flavours to the wine. Four or five days fermentation on the pulp is usually quite sufficient.

There seems to be no advantage in using hard water or soft water. By and large there can be no improvement on the water that comes straight out of the tap. For our purposes it can be regarded as being adequately pure.

The vessel to be used for mashing, i.e., the preparation of the pulp, should be large and light enough for it to be moved freely when full so that the contents are not spilled. The vessel must be such that it can be closely covered to keep out moulds and fungi at all times. Wine should never be left open to the air since this causes oxidation and imparts a flat dull taste to the finished wine. A close fitting plastic lid is quite suitable; so is a closely woven thick cloth which has good overlaps at the side. An active yeast should always be used to start a fermentation but it should never be added until twenty-four hours after the Campden tablet.

When using vegetables, after their preparation they should be thoroughly washed and then gently boiled until they are tender. The liquor is then strained off the vegetable and it is this which is used to make the wine. Before boiling root vegetables they should, of course, be scrubbed clean from any trace of earth and with parsnips, carrots and beetroots, the tops should be cut off close to the vegetable.

When using flowers only the petals should be used and great care should be taken to exclude any green parts of leaf, stalk or calex, because these contain bitter substances which cause most unpleasant flavours in the finished wine.

Whenever citrus fruits are used they should be peeled very thinly with an appropriate knife to ensure that no white pith adheres to the skin. The fruit should then be cut across the centre and all the juice squeezed out. It is only the juice and the thinly pared skin that is used in wine making. The white pith contains a bitter substance which gives an unpleasant flavour to the wine.

After a must has been steeping for several days or has been fermenting on the pulp for a few days all the solids should be extracted. This is done by straining the liquid through a good quality linen cloth or bag and by steadily squeezing the cloth until all the juice is extracted and the fruit pulp is quite dry. This is a fairly laborious but quite essential task. A small hand press removes much of the drudgery and if you intend to make substantial quantities of wine or regularly to make hard fruit wines such as apple, pear, gooseberry, etc., a press is absolutely invaluable. It is usually recommended to place a linen cloth in the press and to place the fruit in the cloth. The lid is then put on to the press and the screw started turning. The screw should not be turned continually, but rather intermittently so that between turns all the juice can be extracted from the last pressure before the pressure is increased. By this means the pulp can be reduced to dryness.

If fermentation has been started on the pulp this is the time to stir in the additional sugar. If fermentation has not yet started the active yeast and nutrient should now be added to the must and the sugar stirred in. Before doing so of course it is important to check the specific gravity to ensure that you add sufficient, but only sufficient, sugar. Fruit quality can vary so much that one year a fruit can contain up to 1 lb of sugar per gallon, whilst in another year the same fruit may yield less than $\frac{1}{2}$ lb sugar per gallon. Having adjusted the must to the specific gravity of your choice – a figure of 1.080 or thereabouts is recommended – the jar should be placed in a warm situation so that fermentation can start or continue without further interruption.

CHAPTER SIX

Fermentation - principles and methods

Although drinks have been fermented for more than 10,000 years, the principles of fermentation have only been properly understood in the last 100 years or so. Until Pasteur conducted his famous experiments in the middle of the nineteenth century it was thought that fermentation was caused by oxygen or an act of God in the form of some spontaneous action. Yeast was known as leaven, and it was understood that it had to be added to cause the fermentation of beer, but the method by which it worked was still a mystery. As a result of further scientific investigation since Pasteur all the details are now clearly understood and the various chemical processes have been fully revealed and explained.

The yeast cell is absolutely essential to fermentation. It is so small that it cannot be seen with the naked eye and end to end some 7,000 measure only 1 in or 2.5 cm. This tiny cell belongs to the vegetable rather than to the animal kingdom and comes in countless varieties and strains. In fermentation at home we are mostly concerned with *Saccharomyces cerevisiae* which is circular in shape and is used mostly in the fermentation of beer and the making of bread. The yeast used for making wine is a variety of this strain called *Saccharomyces ellipsoideus*. As its name implies this is eliptical in shape and is indigenous to the grape. Both varieties have similar characteristics but the *ellipsoideus* tends to have a somewhat higher alcoholic tolerance and settles more firmly on the bottom of a jar or bottle. Furthermore it tends to give the wine a better flavour than that conferred by the *cerevisiae* variety.

The yeast cell secretes a number of enzymes, the two most important of which for our purposes are invertase and the apozymase complex. An enzyme is a protein catalyst and causes a change in a substance simply by its presence. Invertase, for example, splits sucrose, ordinary white granulated sugar, into its two component parts, fructose and glucose. Sucrose is not directly fermentable but both of the simple sugars fructose and glucose are fermentable. The apo-zymase complex of enzymes now takes over, and by their very presence these slightly different enzymes cause the sugars to break down through a complicated chain of processeses into carbon dioxide and alcohol.

The yeast of itself, then, plays no direct part in fermentation, it merely acts as the host for the enzymes which it secretes and which in fact cause the fermentation. This word comes from the French 'fervere' which means to boil. During fermentation the bubbles of carbon dioxide rise to the surface so vigorously that the impression is given of a boiling liquid. In a gallon of a fermenting must there are many millions of yeast cells and the chain of chemical changes is making an excited progression.

The yeast cell needs certain conditions in which to grow, thrive and secrete its enzymes. First it needs an acid solution, this is provided by the acidity of the fruit or by the addition of acid when the fruit is lacking in sufficient acidity. Next the yeast needs a nutrient in the form of nitrogen which it can usually obtain from the fruit mucelage or from the di-ammonium phosphate which we add in small quantities to ensure that the yeast has enough. Finally, plenty of oxygen is needed for reproduction. This is obtained from the oxygen dissolved in the must during the preparation. When fermentation starts it is important to exclude the air both to keep out unwanted microbes of all kinds as well as additional oxygen. By confining the available oxygen to that already dissolved in the must, the rate of reproduction of the yeast is controlled and this reduces the amount of deposit of dead yeast in the jars. Yeast cells reproduce themselves every three hours and die after about thirty reproductions. The dead cells are then decomposed in a process called autolysis. Some further nitrogen is thus made available to the remaining yeast, but other by-products of the decomposition of the yeast impart an unpleasant bouquet and flavour to the wine. This is why it is so important to rack new wine off its lees as soon as fermentation is finished.

Providing the conditions are right the yeast will continue to ferment all the sugar available until it is inhibited from doing so by the quantity of alcohol present. There are seven reasons to cause fermentation to stop. (1) so much alcohol has been formed that the yeast is inhibited from further activity; (2) all the available sugar has been used up, i.e. has been converted into alcohol and carbon dioxide; (3) the solution is insufficiently acid to enable the yeast to act; (4) the liquid contains insufficient nutrient to enable the yeast to act; (5) the carbon dioxide has not been able to escape and has inhibited the yeast from further activity; (6) the temperature of the must is too high and has caused the yeast to become lethargic; (7) the temperature of the must is too low and has caused the yeast to become lethargic.

If a fermenting must stops fermenting, the cause is one of the seven reasons given above. When the cause is lack of acid or nutrient, it is frequently necessary to add a new active yeast at the same time as the additional acid or nutrient. Fermentation is best carried out at a fairly constant temperature of about 70°F. Some yeasts will ferment, albeit slowly, at a very much lower temperature of 50°F. and some yeasts will continue to ferment, albeit slowly, up to about 90°F. Beyond this temperature the yeast not only becomes lethargic but also dies. At 120°F. it is, of course, killed quite quickly.

Most wine yeasts, given the right conditions, can tolerate up to 15 per cent of alcohol. Exceptionally, some will tolerate up to 17 per cent but this is most unusual and any higher percentages should be regarded with scepticism.

Yeasts can be bought in tablet form or as tiny granules, in a liquid form or as culture on an agar jelly grown in a test tube. The yeasts mostly come from abroad and start off as pure cultures taken from a single cell on a grape. These cultures are then grown on and eventually are sold under the name of the type of wine usually made from the grape in that neighbourhood. Accordingly one can buy yeast with names such as Burgundy, Champagne, Sherry, Port, Madeira, Hock, Pommard, Sauterne, etc., etc.

Whilst these yeasts will not convert any must into a wine of that type, there is little doubt that, given a sympathetic must, these yeasts do tend to produce wines similar in character to those whose name they bear. There would be little point in using a Champagne yeast with a Port-like must and vice versa, but if you use ingredients to produce a wine similar in type to that produced by the yeast in its country of origin, then the yeast will impart some of its flavour and characteristics to that wine.

All yeast is best prepared in a starter bottle before use. This ensures that a very active ferment is added to the must and that there will be no delay in starting the fermentation. The yeast starter bottle is quite simple to prepare. Pour half a point of cold, boiled water into a sterile bottle, add a dessertspoonful of sugar, an ounce of fruit juice containing some acid such as orange juice or lemon juice, then add a little yeast nutrient and the yeast of your choice. Plug the neck of the bottle with cotton wool and place the bottle in a warm place about 77°F. Shake the bottle from time to time and within twenty-four hours or so the yeast will become active and the occasional bubble of carbon dioxide will be seen floating to the surface. Within two or three days a really active starter will be prepared and when this is added to the must the whole will be working within twenty-four hours. This helps to ensure that the must is kept wholesome and that it is not impregnated with unwanted bacteria, spores and fungi that constantly float invisibly in the air.

With the aid of an hydrometer the fermentation of a must can be controlled so as to ensure that the right amount of alcohol is produced for the type of wine that you wish to make. An hydrometer is used to measure the difference in weight between one liquid, or rather any given liquid, and water at a temperature of 59°F. Water is used because of its universal availability. The graduation on an hydrometer instrument derives from the fact that a cubic foot of water weighs approximately 1,000 ounces. Accordingly the standard specific gravity is known as 1.000 and the weight of all other liquids is compared with this standard. Obviously a liquid which contains sugar, fruit juice and the like, is heavier than plain water. By reading the hydrometer immersed in the liquid we can tell instantly by how much the liquid is heavier than water, and therefore how much sugar it contains. It has been known in Britain since 1786 and is undoubtedly the most valuable piece of equipment that any winemaker can possess. On the Continent of Europe and in America a different graduation is used but ultimately it gives the same results.

The hydrometer is a thin glass tube with graduation marks on it weighted in a slightly bulbous end. It is used in connection with a trial jar slightly taller than the hydrometer and about 1 in or so in diameter (250–300 mm). The hydrometer is placed into the trial jar which is then filled with the liquid to be tested. When the hydrometer is floating you must look across the top of the liquid at the graduation mark and make a note of the figure. By referring to the tables which follow you can tell how much more sugar to add or how much alcohol you can expect to obtain from the sugar already in the must.

S.G.	Potential per cent alcohol by volume	Amount of sugar in the gall. lb oz		Amount of sugar added to the gall. lb oz		Volume of one gallon with sugar added gall. fl oz	
1010	0.9		2		2½	1	1
1015	1.6		4		5	1	3
1020	2.3		7		8	1	5
1025	3.0		9		10	1	7
1030	3.7		12		13	1	8
1035	4.4		15	1	0	1	10
1040	5.1	1	1	1	2	1	11
1045	5.8	1	3	1	4	1	13
1050	6.5	1	5	1	7	1	14
1055	7.2	1	7	1	9	1	16
1060	7.8	1	9	1	11	1	17
1065	8.6	1	11	1	14	1	19
1070	9.2	1	13	2	1	1	20
1075	9.9	1	15	2	4	1	22
1080	10.6	2	1	2	6	1	23
1085	11.3	2	4	2	9	1	25
1090	12.0	2	6	2	12	1	27
1095	12.7	2	8	2	15	1	28
1100	13.4	2	10	3	2	1	30
1105	14.1	2	12	3	5	1	32
1110	14.9	2	14	3	8	1	33
1115	15.6	3	0	3	11	1	35
1120	16.3	3	2	3	14	1	37
1125	17.0	3	4	4	1	1	38
1130	17.7	3	6	4	4	1	40
1135	18.4	3	8	4	7	1	42

European and American Equivalents

Specific Gravity	Degs. Baume	Degs. Twadell	Degs. Brix
1.005	1.0	1.0	1.6
1.010	1.4	2.0	3.0
1.015	2.2	3.0	4.1
1.020	2.8	4.0	5.3
1.025	3.5	5.0	6.5
1.030	4.2	6.0	7.7
1.035	4.7	7.0	8.8
1.040	5.6	8.0	9.9
1.045	6.2	9.0	11.1
1.050	6.9	10.0	12.3
1.055	7.5	11.0	13.4
1.060	8.2	12.0	14.5
1.065	8.8	13.0	15.7
1.070	9.5	14.0	16.9
1.075	10.0	15.0	18.0
1.080	10.7	16.0	19.2
1.085	11.4	17.0	20.4
1.090	12.0	18.0	21.5
1.095	12.4	19.0	22.6
1.100	13.2	20.0	23.7

The temperature of the liquid to be tested affects the accuracy of hydrometer readings and any substantial variation from the norm of 59°F. should be adjusted with the following table:

Temperature in Degrees		Correction to the last figure of the Specific
Centigrade	*Fahrenheit*	Gravity reading
10	50	Subtract 0.6
15	59	No correction necessary
20	68	Add 0.9
25	77	Add 2.0
30	86	Add 3.4
35	95	Add 5.0
40	104	Add 6.8

The Twadell scale used in America is graduated so that 1° Twadell equals 5° specific gravity.

Fruit juices have a natural sugar and the quantity of this should be checked before adding granulated white sugar. Although a recipe may suggest 3 lb of sugar as being necessary it could well be that the quality of the fruit you are using is so rich in sugar that 2½ lb of sugar will be quite adequate to give you the same results. When starting a fermentation it is often best to begin at a specific gravity of 1.080 or there abouts. This will produce between 10 and 11 per cent of alcohol by volume, which is sufficient for a dry table wine. If it is desired to make the wine any stronger an additional quantity of sugar may be added during fermentation. Experience has shown that fermentation starts easiest at this specific gravity and that in higher regions the weight of the sugar can overlay the yeast and inhibit fermentation. Sugar may be added at any time during fermentation, there is no need to put it all in at the beginning. When additional sugar is added, however, it is important to make sure that it is added in syrup form since the addition of dry sugar crystals to a fermenting must causes substantial forming and therefore loss of wine.

Strong wines are best produced by adding controlled amounts of sugar in syrup form each time the specific gravity falls to say 1.010. By raising the gravity 10° or 15° at a time and continuing fermentation, the alcohol tolerance of the yeast is steadily increased and a strong wine is produced. Furthermore the controlled addition of the sugar ensures that the finished product is not too sweet. A maximum specific gravity of 1.120 is quite adequate for a strong sweet wine.

You will have noticed that the more sophisticated recipes contain a recommended starting specific gravity and alcohol content. Although these can of course be varied you will find them a very useful guide in the preparation of wines of different types for different purposes. Experience has shown that the best kind of sugar to use is the ordinary white granulated sugar. Chemically it is no different from any other kind of sugar; furthermore it is the cheapest avilable and the easiest to use. It is best to dissolve 2 lb of sugar in 1 pint of water and to use this syrup as the necessary additive. Brown sugars tend to give a slightly caramel flavour to wines and should never be used with white wines. They are of course beneficial in the preparation of Madeira-type wines and can also be used with red dessert wines. Malt or honey when used in place of sugar in wine varies the flavour considerably and is not recommended except for specific meads.

During the process of fermentation energy is released and the temperature of the must rises by about 10°F. It is always a little hotter inside the jar than it is outside and this thought should be borne in mind when deciding where to keep the jar during fermentation. A good steady temperature is desirable so that fermentation can continue without interruption. Nevertheless this process can continue from three weeks to three months. In musts that contain a good deal of fruit mucilage there is frequently heavy foaming during the first day or so and unless one is careful a horrible mess can be made all over the floor.

It is not essential to keep the jars full during fermentation since carbon dioxide being heavier than air will lay on top of the must and push out the air. By allowing a small space in the jars fermentation can continue tumultuously at first without causing inconvenience. Subsequently the fermentation will settle down and continue until the sugar has been fermented right out to dryness.

As fermentation slows down the dead yeast cells, fruit mucilage and other waste products fall to the bottom of the jar and form a firm sediment known as lees. It is important to remove the new wine from the lees as quickly as possible to avoid spoilation and this is in fact the beginning of the next process in the making of wine, that of maturation.

CHAPTER SEVEN

Maturing the young wine

As soon as fermentation is finished and the wine begins to clear the jar should be moved to a table and on the floor beneath it should be placed a clean sterile storage jar. The fermentation lock should now be removed from the fermentation jar and one end of a siphon inserted in such a manner that it will not disturb the sediment in the bottom of the jar. The other end of the tube is taken between the finger and thumb and inserted into the mouth. The new wine is sucked into the tube and as soon as it reaches the finger and thumb they should be squeezed together to stop the flow until the mouth of the tube is placed into the neck of the clean storage jar. The wine will now flow steadily into the new jar because the weight of wine in the tube outside the fermentation jar is heavier than the weight of the wine in the tube inside the fermentation jar.

By carefully tilting the fermentation jar it is possible to transfer all the clear wine from that jar to its storage jar beneath; only sediment will remain and this should be washed out and thrown away. If the storage jar is not quite full, it should be filled to the bung either with wine of the same kind or wine of a similar kind. If no wine is available of any kind, then cold boiled water may be used instead. Clearly, however, this dilutes the wine and only very small quantities should be used. If the amount necessary to fill the jar is too great then several smaller jars should be used instead.

At this stage some winemakers use small barrels or casks in which to mature their wine – especially their red wine. Given the right circumstances there is no doubt that wine matures in wood better than in anything else. Unfortunately we suffer from a very humid climate in Great Britain and unless these casks can be stored in a dry atmosphere there is no advantage in using casks over jars.

During its period of maturation in cask the wine suffers a good deal of evaporation. In a drier atmosphere it is the water which evaporates from the wine. In a damp, humid atmosphere unfortunately it is the alcohol which evaporates and so the wine is weakened. In either case it is important to top up the cask every two or three weeks with wine of the same kind or a similar kind. In humid circumstances where there is a fair amount of condensation round about, it is advisable to top up with Polish spirit or Vodka in cold boiled water in the proportion of 1 part Polish spirit to 8 parts water.

The smallest size cask suitable for maturing wine is about 6 gallons. In smaller casks the ratio of the surface of the wine to its volume is such that oxidation of the wine takes place and, instead of improving, the wine deteriorates.

Casks should, of course, always be laid on their sides on cask supports and never stood on their ends, otherwise the upper end wood dries out and air and infection can enter through the cracks and so spoil the wine. By storing the casks on their sides all the wood is kept moist all of the time and the joints are therefore kept airtight. Before being used for storage all casks and jars should of course be thoroughly sterilised. With jars of course it is sufficient to wash them carefully in warm water and to sterilise them with a solution of potassium metabisulphite as already indicated.

Casks are more difficult to clean and to keep clean, but it is absolutely imperative to ensure that they are absolutely clean from all previous sediment, mould or dirt, that they smell sweet to the nose, that they have been carefully sterilised with a metabisulphite solution as previously described. When not in use casks should be kept full of water containing a few grains of citric acid and two Campden tablets to the gallon. They should never be allowed to dry out because once they become contaminated it is almost impossible adequately to sterilise them again.

Experiments are continuing with high density polythene, so far with fairly good results. It is essential to ensure, however, that the polythene has no smell and that the container is thoroughly clean from its previous contents and has been sterilised as already mentioned. Unfortunately the plastic industry is still developing and from time to time, the formulae of the plasticiser used may vary. So what is true of one high density polythene container is not necessarily true of another.

Glass jars are still very popular because they are easy to clean and one can readily see the contents within. Regular examination reveals the clarity of the wine and the amount of deposit formed, thus indicating the need for further racking. Clear glass containers should be shielded from the light with thick brown paper or the like. Light causes red wines to fade and experience shows that all wine matures best when kept in the dark.

For this reason glazed earthenware jars have much to commend them. They are easy to clean and sterilise. They tend to insulate the wine from the temperature around it and so keep it at a steady temperature. They keep out the light, they are easy to seal, and although they are heavy, even when empty, come in a variety of sizes one to six gallons.

During storage wine should be kept in the dark at a steady temperature of around 55°F. if possible and free from vibration. Further chemical changes are continuing during maturation and it is important to provide ideal circumstances for this as far as possible. Jars should be kept clearly labelled with their contents because after a year or so it is terribly difficult to tell one wine from another especially if you have been making a good number of wines both red and white.

Every two to three months the wine should be racked until it is brilliantly clear and throwing no further deposit. After a period of six to eight months in storage, consideration should be given to bottling the wine. If you are satisfied that it is star bright and of good bouquet and flavour, sufficient bottles and corks should be washed and sterilised. Cylindrical corks should be used for preference and these should be soaked in water containing a Campden tablet and a few grains of citric acid. A weight will be necessary on top of the corks to keep them submerged in the liquid. If possible they should be soaked for twenty-four hours, shaken free from the sterilising solution and then rinsed in a little of the wine to be bottled, just prior to corking. The bottles should be washed thoroughly clean and if necessary cleaned with a bottle brush. Sometimes it is necessary to hold a bottle up to the light to ensure that it is perfectly clean. A sterilising solution is then made up as previously described and each bottle is rinsed thoroughly and the contents then poured into the next bottle. Just before filling each bottle the last drains of the sterilising solution should be shaken out.

Bottling is done in the same way as racking. The storage jar is placed on a table and the empty bottles on the floor beneath. A siphon is then placed in the storage jar the free end sucked full of wine and then inserted into the first bottle to be filled. The bottles should be filled just above the bottom of the neck so that when the cork is inserted a gap of about three-quarters of an inch exists between the bottom of the cork and the top of the wine. When inserting the corks it is a good tip to slip a piece of plastic covered wire or a piece of string down the neck of the bottle, to push the cork home and then to remove the piece of string or plastic covered wire. This relieves the air pressure between the bottom of the cork and the top of the wine and saves the cork from being pushed out. A neat fit is thus ensured. The cork can then be dried and waxed or a capsule fitted to encase the top of the cork and the neck of the bottle. The bottle should then be dried and labelled and laid on its side in a store for a further three to six months at least. Experience has shown that this period of bottle age after storage is of tremendous importance in obtaining a wine of good flavour and bouquet. On innumerable occasions the author has noticed quite remarkable improvement in wines during this period of bottle storage.

Care, cleanliness and patience are the keynotes of maturation. Good wines can be ruined during this period, whilst average wines can be enhanced enormously. But when everything possible has been done that can be done, it so happens that for reasons unknown to us some wines turn out better than others. A recipe that made an excellent wine this year, when used the following year can make a wine of only mediocre quality. There are so many variables, such as the land on which the fruit was grown, the weather during the winter and the summer period. The harvesting, and the condition of the fruit when it was actually made into wine. All these can alter and change the quality of wine quite noticeably. Wines that have not turned out as well as you had hoped need not be thrown away or neglected but should be carefully blended together. For reasons which again we do not fully understand, wines that have been blended together tend to lose all their bad faults and take on good characteristics. Most commercial wines have been blended at some time or another, either with other wines of the same neighbourhood in the same year or with wines from other years or both. There is no reason then why we should not do the same and our wines will improve accordingly.

When preparing for a blending session taste a number of wines in different jars and set out those that you feel would benefit from blending. In fact most wines would improve with blending but there is a tendency to keep as single wines those which are superior to others. Blending is best done in a large container such as a large sized plastic tub and the wines to be blended should be carefully poured or siphoned into the container. There is no point in trying to be too specific in what one blends with what. The argument that you should at first blend different wines together in different variations in small quantities until you have found the blend which is better than the others is not really valid. During the period of maturation after blending, wines undergo further chemical changes and not infrequently fermentation begins again. Often cloudy or hazy wines clear and deposits are usually thrown. The finished blended wine then is not necessarily likely to have any similarity with the mixture of wines first tasted.

On the other hand there is no merit in blending all wines of the same kind. The best principle to observe is to blend opposites. An excessively dry wine can be blended with one that is rather too sweet. One lacking in tannin can be blended with one that is rather harsh. Wines that are over acid can be blended with wines that are lacking acid. Wines that are very strong in flavour can be blended with wines that are rather tasteless. Blends need not be confined to two wines but may very well contain five or six totally different wines sometimes of different colours. The author has frequently made quite superb rosé wines by this method.

When all the wines are in the container they should be gently stirred about to ensure that they are thoroughly mixed. Then siphon the blend either into clean storage jars or into clean bottles and store for six to eight weeks while the wines homogenise. There is no doubt that you will be immensely pleased with the results and having used your ingenuity in making such a splendid wine you should now exercise the same gift on thinking of a suitable name for your wine.

Wine has such a helpful and beneficial effect on mankind that it is quite exceptional for anything to go wrong in the making.

Wine racks in which to mature and store the finished wine

A thermostatically controlled immersion heater in a polythene pail. Ideal for mashing grain beers at the right temperature, or for maintaining a steady fermentation temperature when making wine

Ideal jars for beer. Can be served straight from the tap to the glass

Perhaps the most common failing is a slight taste of acetic acid or vinegarishness. This is due to the must not having been properly sulphited in the preparation stage, to the vessel not having been kept closely covered at all times to keep out infection, to the use of a vessel which has been contaminated with vinegar, or to vinegar having been used in the same room as the wine has been made. For example, if you intend to pickle onions or make chutney, to souse herrings or the like, in a room in which wine is in any stage of preparation or fermentation or maturation, then the wine will pick up the strong taint of vinegar and it will be noticeable in the finished product. Unfortunately there is no cure at all for this ailment but it is one that can be so easily prevented by proper hygiene and a little thoughtful care that there is no reason at all why it should ever happen.

The next most common ailment is an off-flavour in the finished wine due to insufficient racking after fermentation and during the early part of storage. Because the dead yeast cells are de-composing it is most important to remove them, and decomposing fruit pulp cells as well, from the finished wine. Wine should never be allowed to stand on its lees and as soon as a sediment is noticeable the wine should be racked into a clean storage jar. Frequent rackings help to clarify a wine and the occasional use of 1 Campden tablet per gallon will assist in stabilising and sterilising a finished wine.

Haziness is probably the most common problem, although the vast majority of wines clear naturally by themselves. If a pectic destroying enzyme has been used during preparation the possibility of haze in a finished wine is greatly reduced. Except in cereal wines, starch haze is unlikely to be encountered and provided no metal is ever used or allowed to come into contact with the wine metallic hazes can always be avoided. Occasionally, however, a yeast will decline to settle firmly on the bottom and one is tempted to filter the wine or take some such similar action. Filtering is rarely a satisfactory method since the wine passes so slowly through the filter that it oxodises and the last position is worse than the first. Several proprietary fining agents are available on the market and should be used in accordance with their manufacturers' instructions.

The white of egg beaten up in wine, however, has been found to be as effective as anything else and a good deal cheaper. The white of one egg beaten in half a pint of wine and then thoroughly

D

mixed into the wine to be cleared is sufficient to clear 5 gallons. After having stirred the beaten egg-white into the wine leave it to settle for a few days and within a week a thick deposit will usually be seen on the bottom of the jar.

A substance called Bentonite had long been known for its splendid fining qualities, but until recently it has not been generally available in Britain in small quantities. Happily it is now available from a number of our suppliers at a cost of about 25p per lb. ⅛ oz is ample to clear 1 gallon of wine. Before using the Bentonite it has to be suspended in hot though not boiling water in the proportion of 1½ oz water to ⅛ oz Bentonite powder. It is easier to mix it in larger quantities than small and the simplest method so far discovered is to pour 12 oz of hot water into a bottle, add 1 oz of the Bentonite powder, screw in or on a stopper – this is much preferable to a cork – and shake the bottle vigorously up and down as you would if you were mixing a cocktail. Leave the bottle for 2 or 3 days at least giving it a shake every now and then. The liquid will keep for months.

When the suspended Bentonite is ready for use, rack your wine to remove any sediment from the jar, shake up your Bentonite suspension and pour one-eighth of the quantity, i.e. about 1½ tablespoonsful into each jar to be cleared. Replace the bung and slowly swirl the jar in a circular motion so that the Bentonite is thoroughly dispersed throughout the wine. Rigorous action should always be avoided since this shakes up the wine to its detriment As soon as the Bentonite is well dispersed throughout the wine, return the jar to store and leave for four weeks so that the suspended Bentonite may not only fall to the bottom of the jar but may pack down reasonably tightly on the base. This sediment is highly flocculent, however, and lifts with the least disturbance. Great care must therefore be taken when racking the star bright wine from the sediment, to ensure that it is not disturbed in any way. It may not in fact be possible to get quite as much wine from the jar as you would normally do. The wine should be stored for a further 6 months before bottling it.

Wine is normally clear after the first racking after storage for two months and finings should not be used unless the wine is quite cloudy after six months. If you always add a pectin destroying enzyme such as Pectolase of Pectinol when preparing your must, you will not have pectin hazes in your finished wine. The omission of this ingredient is perhaps the most common cause of wine haze, and if you follow the recommendations set out then the problem can be avoided.

Pectin, as you know, is the 'setting' substance in jam-making. Unless it is destroyed by a pectin destroying enzyme, infinitely small globules of a jelly-like substance are formed and trap the waste particles of fruit that normally settle without difficulty. The microscopic jelly-like globules protect these haze particles from other fining agents and from settling by themselves. If you have forgotten to add a pectin destroying enzyme when preparing your must and you have a hazy wine as a result you should use three times the normal dose, i.e. 3 teaspoonful per gallon and stand the jar in a warm place for a few days. If necessary Bentonite can then be used to help clear the wine.

Happily, Bentonite does not affect the wine and is not injurious in any way.

Pectin destroying enzymes tend to be inhibited by sugar so should be added to the must prior to the addition of the sugar.

Very occasionally one comes across a condition called ropiness in which the wine develops a slimy feel and a sheen in appearance. This is due to long chains or ropes of bacteria which are usually members of the bacteria gracile family, this being the family name covering a variety of similar bacteria, sometimes know as lactic acid bacteria. Happily the ailment has a simple remedy. Two Campden tablets per gallon should be dissolved in the wine which should then be beaten thoroughly with a wooden spoon to break up the ropes or chains of bacteria. After a thorough beating and sterilisation with the potassium metabisulphite, the wine will throw a sediment from which the clean bright wine should be racked as soon as possible into a thoroughly clean and sterilised jar. After three or four weeks the wine will have completely recovered and will be perfectly suitable for drinking.

Occasionally a bad cork can affect a wine and in this connection it is important to use the best corks that you can obtain and to sterilise them thoroughly before use. Corks should always be stored in a clean dry place away from any damp and dirt.

Jars not in use should be washed thoroughly, then sterilised and after they have been thoroughly dried plugged with cotton wool. The same applies to bottles and all vessels and equipment. Everything used in winemaking should be kept thoroughly clean and dry at all times. Rust and mould develop wherever there is dirt and damp. Spores and fungi cannot develop in clean dry sterilised conditions. Simple kitchen hygiene together with the regular use of sulphite as already indicated will prevent immense effort in trying to clean soiled vessels and equipment and trying to put right wines that that have gone wrong. When making wine, as with cooking, wash your hands frequently, keep any spilt wine wiped up with a cloth impregnated with sulphite. If wine should get spilled in the wine store mop it up immediately and wipe the surface clean with sulphite. The old proverb 'a stitch in time saves nine' is as true in winemaking as it is in everything else. The emphasis on cleanliness and the use of sulphite cannot be over emphasised.

There is always talk of how long a wine should be kept before it is served. The answer is different with every wine. No two wines ever need precisely the same period of time. Light wines develop more quickly than heavier wines. Wines that contain much acid, tannin or alcohol will keep for longer periods than wines that have less quantities. In general terms the author is of the opinion that the earliest at which a wine can be drunk is nine months after making it and that most wines will continue to improve for several years. Many red wines simply are not ready for drinking until at least two years after they are made and this applies especially to strong and rich wines. On the other hand there is no real evidence to show that wines made in small quantities in the home will go on improving for ever. Twenty-five years experience indicate that most wines are at their best when they are between eighteen months and two and a half years old and only very few wines are worth keeping up to four years. But drinking is the subject of another chapter and when a wine is really ready for drinking it has finished its period of maturation.

CHAPTER EIGHT

How to brew good beer

Of all the different hobbies few have developed quite so fast as that of making beer at home. Every conceivable aid to the home brewer is available so that he can follow faithfully the processes of commercial brewers. But for those who want quick and easy methods countless packs are available that need little more than water and perhaps some sugar.

What is often overlooked is that home-made beer can so easily be made so strong as to cause embarrassment to those with no background knowledge of the subject. Naturally people are in business to sell their wares. It is up to the individual to know their own capacity to consume the result. It is no part of the business man's duty to give warnings of the potentcy of home-made beer nor to advise moderation or caution. He is offering an excellent commodity at a reasonable price. He cannot be blamed for advertising its worth. And yet people who have not made beer before and who have perhaps rarely drunk beer, buy these packs. They do not always follow the recipe faithfully and frequently drink the results in a manner, that may well cause drunkenness with its associated risks to personal safety.

Home-brewed beer, properly made and matured is a superb beverage, beneficial as a tonic, perfect as an accompaniment to certain foods and a wonderful aid to relaxation and enjoyment of fellowship. When well made it can be superior to most commercially prepared beers. Even an average brew is as good as can be bought.

There is a tendency for the beginner to brew beer at home much stronger than is necessary or desirable and to drink it by the quart and more, sometimes on an empty stomach. Such a person would probably never contemplate drinking two or three bottles of wine or half a bottle of whisky at a sitting. They would know what to expect, but they seem to think that home-made beer is no more alcoholic than a mild commercial beer.

There have been a few newspaper reports of calamities caused by drinking home-brewed beer and it would be a tragedy if the hobby were to get a bad name or result in the imposition of taxation.

At present a pint of the best beer can be brewed at home for less than 2½p per pint. There are no wages costs, brewers' overheads, taxes, distribution costs, nor publicans' wages and overheads. But at any time a penal tax could be imposed on the ingredients so that brewing beer at home would lose much of its special appeal.

The purpose of this chapter then, is not only to provide information on how to brew beer at home, but also to indicate clearly how to brew it and drink it to ensure maximum satisfaction and enjoyment.

All the Western European countries are great beer brewers and drinkers. Denmark, of course, is famous for its lager, a drink now becoming very popular in Britain. Beer is traditionally an Englishman's drink for we have been brewing and drinking it since before the Romans offered us the hop to flavour our brew, but for more than 1,000 years we refused to use it, preferring instead the nettle and other herbs. WE called our brew ale and used the Teutonic word 'bier' to name a hopped ale.

Knowledge of our beverage during this period comes through the writings of Roman historians – most of whom didn't think much of it and preferred wine. Its potentcy was known and in the 5th Century the monk Gildas decreed that 'If any monk through drinking too freely gets thick of speech so that he cannot join the psalmody, he is to be deprived of his supper'. In the 6th Century St David restated this law with stricter penalties. At the end of the 7th Century Theodore the 7th Archbishop of Canterbury extended the law to laymen. But Alwin an 8th Century scholar clearly indicated that sin lay not in the use, but in the abuse of alcoholic liquor. His words are just as true today.

By the 9th Century ale houses were becoming common in town and village. At first these were huts adjacent or built on to the house where the ale was brewed for sale to travellers. The availability of ale for sale was indicated by a pole – the forebears of modern inn signs. If wine was also sold an evergreen bush was attached to the pole.

At the end of the 10th Century and the beginning of the 11th we have written evidence of rent for land being paid in ale. Presumably land-holding peasants brewed their own. At least it is also clear that those who brewed ale, paid part of their rent in ale. The latin word used to describe them was CEREVISIARII derived from CEREVISIAE which is the term now given to the variety of yeast used for brewing beer.

Other local tithes payable in ale developed and in 1188 Henry II imposed the first national tax on ale. Every king and every government ever since has seen fit to tax ale and beer with an increasing burden.

In the following year a law was made in London by the City Council prohibiting the burning by night of reeds, straw or stubble by bakers and 'ale wives'. At this time and for several hundred years to come most of the brewing and selling of ale was done by women. Later on as breweries developed and sold ale to inns and hostelries, what might be termed independent brewing declined. As a result the work was undertaken by men and women turned their hands to other tasks. Within the last few years many women have returned to their former task and some of the best beer being brewed at home is being made by women. Perhaps they hope to keep their husbands with them at home instead of being left alone whilst the men go to their 'local'.

By the end of the 14th Century ale-conners or ale tasters were appointed to inspect each brew and pronounce on its quality. No doubt this was mainly done by the eye, nose and palate, but it was fairly common for the ale conners to wear leather breeches and sit for half an hour in a pool of ale poured on to a wooden bench. If his breeches stuck to the wood when he began to get up, then here was a clear indication that the ale was too sugary and therefore badly fermented.

In addition to the quality the authorities were equally concerned with the quantity. About this time – still the end of the 14th Century – many laws were decreed by City and Town Aldermen and Councillors concerning the official sizes of gallons, quarts and pints as well as barrels. It was not uncommon for a tankard to be used holding 2, 4 or 8 pints at a time. They were made mostly of wood or pewter by the Guild of Coopers who were also responsible for making the barrels.

By the middle of the 15th Century hops were being imported from the Continent and used by progressive brewers not only to improve the flavour of their ale but also to lengthen its life a little. The traditional ale makers put up a valiant fight to keep out the hop and retain the purity of English ale. The new beer was quite popular in the south, however, and gradually became accepted everywhere. Early in the 16th Century hops were planted in Kent and slowly the word ale dropped out of use and was replaced with the word beer.

Fundamentally the brewing industry was now established. As travellers got around they found that the beer in some places tasted better than in others. It was realised that this was due to the water and over the generations certain towns developed a reputation for the quality of their beers due to the minerals or lack of them in the spring or well water which was used in their breweries. For example Burton-on-Trent became famous for its bitter beers, pale, crisp and fresh. On the other hand London became famous for its brown beers and stouts, soft and full.

Scientific research has enabled techniques to be improved. Sterility of vessels and purity of ingredients with quality control at all stages now ensures a beer that will keep, travel and taste good in any part of the world.

The result of these years of research and study are now available to the home brewer. To obtain the best results, only the finest quality ingredients should be used even if they cost a little more. Having regard to the savings on wages and overheads the little extra cost of materials is negligible in relation to the improvement in quality so obtained.

Nearly every town has its 'Home Brew Supplier' and many chemists also carry a wide range of ingredients and equipment.

The basic ingredients of beer are malt, hops, water, sugar and yeast, but there are a number of ancillary items that may be used. Lactose or milk sugar is used for sweetening stouts. Hardening salts are useful in making bitter beers and heading liquid helps to retain the rich creamy head caused by the priming.

Malt is available in several forms. That used by the brewer is a grain which may be lightly, moderately or heavily roasted to give different depths of colour and flavour. It can be purchased by the lb or in larger quantities. It is essential to use grain to make the very best beers.

Very popular is malt extract, a dark treacly substance available in 1 lb and larger containers. It is important to buy a brewing quality where possible. It is essential to buy one free from additions such as cod liver oil. It is quick and easy to use and produces a good average quality beer.

Malt flour is also available and can be obtained in the same varieties as grains. It also makes a good average beer and is quick and easy to use.

Hops are available in different varieties such as Goldings or Fuggles. They need to be fresh since they deteriorate with age becoming very dry, pale and brittle, having lost their oiliness and strong odour.

Goldings are best used for bitter beers, whilst Fuggles are more suitable for brown ales and stouts.

Tap water is perfectly pure and suitable for beer. If you want to brew accurately a variety of different types then you should obtain from your local Water Board the analysis of the mineral content of your water so that you can harden or soften it as may be necessary for your purpose. Bitter beers need about 70 grains calcium sulphate and 10 grains of magnesium sulphate. Brown beers and stouts need no sulphate but benefit from 10 grains of sodium chloride (common salt) .

Granulated yeast would seem to be the most popular form in use for brewing. It is often available in little sachets combined with a yeast energiser. It can also be bought in liquid form and sometimes you can obtain fresh brewer's yeast from a local brewery. It is most important to use this within a day or so whilst still fresh, since it deteriorates rapidly if kept for a week or so even in a refrigerator.

Some home brewers, like their commercial counterparts, pad out their brews with adjuncts. These are grains other than malted barley. Flaked maize, flaked rice, or flaked oatmeal may be used, but never in a quantity amounting to more than 10 per cent of the barley. The adjuncts provide a little more body and flavour. The maize is often used in making bitter beer, the rice is frequently added to brown ales and the oatmeal is sometimes added to stout.

Sugar too, is frequently added sometimes with caramel to darken the brew. Invert sugar is used commercially to ensure rapid and total fermentation but ordinary granulated sugar may be used with just as good results since time is of less importance to the home brewer. Sugar is cheaper than malt and increases the quantity of alcohol produced. For light ales use not more than 10 per cent of the weight of the malt, for bitters not more than 15 per cent and for stouts not more than 20 per cent.

Clearing agents such as isinglass or Carageen moss are sometimes added to ensure a brilliant beer quickly. The author has never found this necessary, however. The beer will clear naturally if left standing for a few days.

METHOD

There are two fundamentally different ways of brewing beer. The easiest is to use a malt extract, the other is to mash the malted barley grains in a way similar to the commercial brewer.

HOW TO MAKE MALT EXTRACT BEERS

PALE ALE

Ingredients

1 lb malt extract
8 oz demerara sugar
1 oz hops
7 pints water
½ teaspoonful granulated yeast

Method

1 Dissolve the malt extract and sugar in 4 pints warm water, add the hops and boil vigorously for 1 hour. Use a large saucepan with a good fitting lid, so that as little steam is lost as possible.

2 At the end of the hour remove the pan from the heat and allow it to stand for five or ten minutes to cool slightly.

3 Strain the liquor through a nylon sieve into a fermenting vessel.

4 Pour a quart of warm water over the hops to wash out the sweetness adhering to them and strain again.

5 Pour a further pint of water over the hops in the same way, and strain again.

6 If necessary make the total quantity up to about 8½ points.

7 As soon as the wort is cool, check the specific gravity with an hydrometer. A reading of between 1.030 and 1.034 is required.

8 Stir in the yeast granules, cover the vessel and leave it to ferment, preferably in a temperature of about 65°F.

9 After two days skim off the yeast head. After about 5 days fermentation will cease.

10 Stir the beer well and pour it in to a narrow-necked jar to which an air lock can be fitted. Move the jar to a cool place and leave it to stand for 3 or 4 days so that the beer can clear.

11 Siphon into 8 clean 1 pint beer bottles and add a level teaspoonful of sugar to each.

12 Fit a crown stopper or screw down a stopper with a new rubber ring.

13 Shake each bottle to dissolve the sugar and store the bottles in a warm place 60–65°F. for five days to encourage bottle fermentation.

14 Move the bottles to a cool store so that the beer can mature. It may be drunk the following week but will keep for three months and improve all the time.

15 Handle the bottle carefully before and during the pouring of the beer. Have your glasses handy and take care to pour the beer down the side of the glass without inverting the bottle from the near horizontal. In this way you can pour perfectly bright beer and leave the sediment behind in the bottle.

The following variations make attractive alternatives.

BITTER BEER

1½ lb malt extract
4 oz pale malt grains
2 oz flaked maize
4 oz sugar
1½ oz Golding hops
7 pints water
Beer yeast

If needs be adjust S.G. to between 1.038 and 1.042.

BROWN ALE

1 lb malt extract
4 oz malt grains
2 oz flaked rice
8 oz brown sugar
1 oz Fuggles hops
2 oz lactose
7 pints water
Beer yeast

An S.G. of between 1.038 to 1.042 is appropriate. Dissolve the lactose in a little beer and return to the jar just before fermentation ends. It will not ferment but will impart a slight sweetness to the ale.

OATMEAL STOUT
1½ lb malt extract
½ lb black malt grains
½ lb flaked oatmeal
½ lb soft brown sugar
1½ oz Fuggles hops
7 pints water
Pinch of salt
Beer yeast

An S.G. of between 1.048 and 1.052 is necessary.

MILK STOUT
1 lb malt extract
½ lb crystal malt grains
¼ lb black malt grains
½ lb soft brown sugar
1½ oz Fuggles hops
7 pints water
Beer yeast
Pinch of salt

4–6 oz lactose (to suit the sweetness of your palate). S.G. as for oatmeal stout.

LAGER TYPE
1½ lb malt extract
1 lb pale malt grains
½ lb white sugar
1 oz Hallertau hops
7 pints water
Lager yeast (*Sacharomyces carlsbergensis*)

S.G. 1.046 to 1.050 is desired. Ferment in a cool place (54°F.). Mature for at least two months.

COCK ALE

This is a favourite recipe of the author and is strongly recommended.

1 lb malt extract
2 oz golden syrup
8 oz demerara sugar
2 oz crystal malt grains
1 oz Golding hops
7 pints water
½ pint white wine
Beer yeast

Wings, bones and oddments of cooked chicken. Prepare the beer as usual. Crush the chicken bones, cut up the chicken and pour on half a pint of dry white wine, such as rhubarb. Cover the vessel and leave to stand for twenty-four hours. When the beer has been fermenting thirty-six hours strain the wine into the beer. Put the chicken and bones into a muslin cloth and add this to the beer. Continue fermentation in a warm place and after three days remove the muslin bag of chicken, squeezing out the liquor. Finish the beer in the usual way and don't forget the priming sugar. Mature for two months.

HOW TO MAKE GRAIN MASHED BEERS
LIGHT ALE
Ingredients
1½ lb crushed pale malted barley
2 oz flaked maize
4 oz demerara sugar
1 gallon water
1 oz Golding hops
Beer yeast

Method
1 Preferably buy malt grains already crushed. If these cannot be obtained crush the grains as best you can with a rolling pin.
2 Heat 6 pints of water to about 165°F., add the malt, maize and sugar, stir well, check the temperature and adjust it to 152°F.
3 Cover the vessel with insulating material such as a fibre glass quilt, old blankets or the like and leave it to stand for 15 minutes.
4 Stir again, check the temperature, adjust to 152°F., replace the insulation and leave for 30 minutes.
5 Repeat the process and leave for a final 15 minutes.
6 Strain the liquor into another vessel and wash the grains with

a quart of water at 165 to 170°F. The hot water can be poured from a kettle and the grains agitated as you do so. This will ensure that no sugar is wasted.

7 Add the hops and boil the liquor vigorously for 1 hour to extract the hop oils and flavour and to coagulate the proteins.

8 Strain the liquor off the hops and wash them with 1 pint of tepid water to remove any syrup that may be clinging to them.

9 Cool the liquor as quickly as possible and when it reaches 58°F., check the S.G. which should be between 1.038 and 1.042. Adjust if necessary.

10 Stir in an active beer yeast and ferment for 5 or 6 days, removing the yeast head on the second day!

11 When fermentation finishes stir the beer well and leave it closely covered for a few days for the sediment to settle.

12 Rack into clean beer bottles and add 1 teaspoonful sugar to each pint of beer.

13 Fix crown corks or screw stoppers and place the bottles in a warm position for the secondary fermentation.

14 Remove the bottles to a cool storage for up to two months.

Alternative recipes may be used to brew different kinds of beers as indicated in the section for making malt extract beers. Or perhaps, more important, the basic recipe can be adjusted to suit your own particular palate. You can add more hops or more malt, omit the maize and add more sugar and so on. Always use at least 1½ lb malt grains to a gallon of water. The mashing system described should give you a yield of maltose equivalent to an S.G. of 1.024 per lb of malt per gallon. So 1½ lb malt will give you a starting S.G. of 1.036. As far as possible use at least 75 per cent malt grains to 15 per cent sugar and 10 per cent adjuncts. You can of course omit the sugar and maize. The sugar is only added to eke out the malt and the maize gives a somewhat drier finish to a pale ale or bitter beer.

CHAPTER NINE

Meads you can make at any time

Traditionally, mead is an Olde Englishe beverage which we associate mainly with the Anglo Saxons. Indeed, there is a story that our word 'honeymoon' comes from the festivities which followed an Anglo Saxon wedding. The story is that the festivities continued for a month, with the drinking of mead each night – hence 'honeymoon'. Be that as it may, mead is certainly a very ancient drink, older even than wine itself.

Mead was well known to the ancient Greek civilisation. Grapes were grown and wine was made from them, but alas the wines were often of poor quality and the Greeks endeavoured to make the drinks more palatable by adding honey and spices. They also used fir cones for flavouring and preserving their wine. As well as mixing honey with grape wine, the Greeks frequently steeped different fruits in mead, i.e., the fermented honey and water, to achieve yet further variations. Many of the words which we use to describe these drinks today have a Greek origin, and some of these very ancient recipes follow in this chapter.

Just as different varieties of grapes grown in different parts of the world make different wines, so do different honeys gathered by bees from different flowers make different meads. You get quite a different mead made from a honey where the bees feed on English clover or Californian orange blossom than you do from a honey where the bees feed on Australian eucalyptus. The latter has a most distinctive flavour, which many people do not find very palatable.

Pale honey, of a creamy colour and texture, usually makes a much better mead than the dark honey, which although thin and runny, often has a much stronger flavour. Because of its innate sweetness, mead usually tastes better if the fermentation is finished just before the mead reaches total dryness, i.e., when all the sugar has been fermented into alcohol and carbon dioxide. Although the specific gravity of a dry wine can be as low as 0.990 it is better if mead is not served lower than 1.000. The flavour is sometimes so delicate that it needs a very slightly sweet background to show it off to its best advantage. Unfortunately, neither light nor dark honey contains any acid or tannin to speak of, so these essential ingredients must always be added.

Honey doesn't contain any natural yeast nutrient either, so it is most important to add double the quantity normally used in making wine, to ensure a satisfactory fermentation of honey.

An analysis of honey shows that in spite of the different flavours, the basic chemical composition remains much as follows :

Sugar 77 per cent Water $17\frac{1}{2}$ per cent

The remaining $5\frac{1}{2}$ per cent includes salts of iron, phosphorous, lime, sodium, potassium, sulphur and managanese, with traces of formic, malic, succinic and amino acids, together with dextrine, pollen, oils, gums, waxes, yeasts, enzymes, vitamins, albumen, protein and ash.

A light sweet mead can be made and drunk in six weeks or so, and the author has tasted and enjoyed such a mead on more than one occasion, and made by different people, too. Indeed he was judging the mead classes in a Show one day and awarded first prize to a particularly fragrant and delicious mead, one that was a joy both to the nose and to the palate. When he was later on introduced to the winner, he congratulated him and was amazed to be told that the mead was in fact only six weeks old. On another occasion the author had entered a two-year-old sweet mead of some character in a Show and was awarded second prize. Upon enquiry he found that the mead which had taken the first prize was only two months old, though made by a different person from the one mentioned above.

In general terms, however, experienced mead makers are agreed that mead is usually very slow in fermenting and maturing especially if it contains more than 10 per cent of alcohol or is made from dark honey. Quite often mead will ferment so slowly that it will continue for from six to twelve months. Clearly such a mead will need three to four years maturation to reach its prime.

If the mead tastes a little too dry when you are about to serve it, you may dissolve a dessertspoonful of light honey in a bottleful of mead. The aroma and sweetness of the honey will add greatly to the pleasure that the mead will otherwise afford you. Mead should always be served cool, since this brings out the bouquet and the flavour to the fullest advantage.

There is some divergence of opinion as to whether honey should be heated to sterilise it and get rid of wax and impurities. On one side this is argued as important to the production of a sound and pleasant mead with good keeping qualities. On the other hand, heating is thought to drive off some of the subtler flavours. If you are making mead from honey produced by your own bees, it may be well to sterilise it gently first. If you are using commercially produced honey, it has probably already been sterilised. It is therefore sufficient to stir your honey into water just warm enough to dissolve it thoroughly. When the liquid is cool, one Campden tablet to the gallon should be added to inhibit the growth of any unwanted bacteria or fungi.

If it is necessary to sterilise the honey, first pour some warm water into a preserving pan or large saucepan. The honey should then be stirred into the warm water until it is dissolved. The liquid may now be brought to the boil very gently and simmered for not more than a quarter of an hour. This causes a rather dirty scum to arise but it can be skimmed off easily and should be thrown away. Make sure that you keep stirring the honey until it is entirely disolved and ensure that none sticks to the bottom of the pan and burns. This would cause a most unpleasent flavour in the mead.

When the honey solution is cool, the acid, nutrient, tannin and yeast should be added and the fermentation started. It is imperative to keep your mead must in a warm place so that the fermentation is not interrupted by the cold. When fermentation has finished rack the mead into a clean jar and after three months rack it again, adding one Campden tablet to the gallon to keep it stabilised so that it does not re-ferment. Six months later bottle the mead, cork it tightly and mature it in a cool place until it is ready for drinking. Always serve it cool and crisp. It may be served whenever you would otherwise serve a white table wine. Dry meads are excellent with fish and with chicken, and sweet mead is quite delicious when served with the dessert. It is also extremely palatable when served with a shortbread biscuit.

Mead is something of an acquired taste, however, and is not

E

liked by everyone. If you have made some mead which you subsequently find that you do not like very much, do not throw it
away but blend it with fruit wines in the proportion of four of
wine to one of mead. This frequently enhances the wine out of all
recognition whilst the taste of mead that you did not like is happily
lost.

Recipes to make 6 bottles (1 gallon) of mead :

TABLE MEAD
Ingredients

3–3½ lbs light honey dissolved in 6½–7 pints of warm water
(140°F.) to make up to 8½ pints of must at a specific gravity of
about 1.090. (Note. The extra ½ pint will allow for wastage when
racking)
Half a cup of cold strong tea
An active Maury or Sherry yeast
½ oz citric acid
1 nutrient tablet

Method

1 Thoroughly dissolve the honey by stirring it in the warm water.
2 As soon as it is cool enough, i.e. about 75°F. stir in and dissolve
all the other ingredients.
3 Fit an airlock to the fermentation jar and stand it in a warm
place. (70–75°F.)
4 As soon as fermentation is finished and the mead begins to clear,
rack it from the lees into a clean storage jar.
5 Top the jar up to the bung with some other mead or with a
light white wine or some cold boiled water.
6 Store the mead in a cool place for three months then rack it
into another clean storage jar. Add one Campden tablet, bung the
jar tight and return it to the store for a further six months.
7 Bottle the mead and keep for a further six months in bottle
before serving.

DESSERT MEAD
Ingredients

4–4½ lb honey dissolved in about six pints of warm water to make
up to 8½ pints at a specific gravity of 1.120
Half a cup of cold strong tea
Maury or Sherry yeast

¾ oz citric acid
1½ nutrient tablets

Method

1 Prepare and ferment as already indicated.
2 When fermentation appears to be coming to an end check the S.G. and if it is below 1.010 add enough honey or sugar to bring it up to about 1.015. An ounce of sugar or 1¾ oz honey raises the gravity about two degrees.
3 If the mead continues to ferment so much the better; continue the additions of sugar or honey as may be necessary to finish the fermentation between 1.015 and 1.018.
4 Rack and mature as already mentioned bearing in mind that this mead will take longer to mature than the table mead because it contains a good deal more alcohol.

SPARKLING MEAD

Ingredients

4 lb of light honey in about 6 pints of water to make up to 8½ pints at an S.G. of 1.110
Half a cup of cold strong tea
Champagne yeast
¾ oz citric acid
1½ nutrient tablets

Method

1 Make as for table mead, rack and keep for three months.
2 When the mead is star bright rack it into Champagne bottles, add ½ oz of honey to each bottle, cork the bottles tightly and wire down the corks. (Note. Dissolve 3 oz honey in a little mead and pour an equal portion into each of the bottles.)
3 Mature the mead in bottle for at least one year and preferably longer, and serve this quite delicious drink cool and fresh.

CYSER

This is a mixture of honey and apple juice. Use the recipe on page 105 for Apple Wine, using 3 lb of honey instead of the sugar.

MELOMEL

This is a mixture of mixed fruits and honey. Use the recipe on page 15 for Mixed Fruit Wine but replace 1½ lb of sugar with 2 lb of honey.

PYMENT

This is a mixture of honey and grape juice fermented and matured.

1 You can use the recipe for table mead adding ½ pint of grape juice concentrate to the honey when dissolving it in the warm water and then follow the method for making Table Mead.

2 You can use the recipe for Raisin Wine on page 110 but use 1½ lb honey instead of the sugar.

3 Or you can make a grape wine as shown on page 113 but add 1 lb of light honey to the grape must half way through the fermentation.

HYPOCRAS I

This is a mixture of spiced grape wine and honey. It gets its name from Hypocrates of ancient medical fame who is said to have strained the wine through the sleeve of his gown to remove the various spices.

Ingredients

1 pint grape juice concentrate
2 lb of light honey
1 gallon of warm water
½ oz of bruised root ginger
12 cloves
1 blade of mace
The rind and juice of three large lemons
1 cup of cold strong tea
1 nutrient tablet
Maury yeast

Method

1 Thoroughly dissolve the honey and the grape juice concentrate in the warm water.

2 Add the lemon juice, the cold tea, the nutrient tablet and the yeast. Put the bruised root ginger, the cloves and the blade of mace, together with the lemon rind in a muslin bag and suspend it in the must.

3 Ferment, rack and nature as already indicated.

4 If it is not sweet enough for your palate when serving, then dissolve a large teaspoonful of honey in one bottle of wine.

HYPOCRAS II

Ingredients

2 lb Californian orange blossom honey (or similar light variety)
$\frac{1}{2}$ lb sultanas
$\frac{1}{2}$ lb white sugar
3 large fresh lemons
$\frac{1}{4}$ teaspoonful of grape tannin
1 nutrient tablet
7 pints water
Champagne yeast

Method

1 Dissolve the honey and sugar in tepid water and pour into a mashing vessel.
2 Wash, chop and add the sultanas to the must.
3 Thinly pare the lemons, halve them, squeeze out the juice and add the peel and juice to the must. Discard the pithy pulp.
4 Stir in an active yeast, the nutrient and the tannin.
5 Cover the vessel, place in the warm and ferment for 5 days, then strain out the solids and ferment under an air lock.
6 Rack and store as usual. Keep for 12 months in jar, then bottle and keep for a further 6 months.
7 Serve chilled, sweetened with a teaspoonful of honey if desired.

METHEGLIN

Ingredients

$3\frac{1}{2}$ lb honey dissolved in $6\frac{1}{2}$ pints of water
$\frac{1}{2}$ lb demerrara sugar
$\frac{1}{2}$ oz of root ginger
12 cloves
1 blade of mace
Rind and juice of 3 large lemons
1 cup of cold strong tea
1 nutrient tablet
Maury yeast

Method

Make in the same way as Hypocras I.
Metheglin like Hypocras needs to be served rather sweet at about S.G. 1.010 or above. If necessary it can be sweetened just prior to serving.

spec grav. 1.01

All fruit meads need to be served medium sweet and a specific gravity of about 1.010 seems to be right for most people. Unless you have an exceptionally cultivated palate for these drinks, their flavour when dry is not nearly so pleasant as when slightly sweet. They are obviously very nutritious as well as delightful drinks, and if you have access to honey at a reasonably price they are well worth making. Imported honey can often be bought at about half the price of English honey especially if you are willing to take a fair quantity of say 14 lb or more at a time.

Everyone who makes wine or beer at home should certainly try to make mead on at least one occasion, if only to continue the tradition of making and drinking this most ancient drink of all.

CHAPTER TEN

Serving wine to its best advantage

Inevitably you will find that you put a great effort into making the very best wine you can. It would be a great pity then, to spoil it by not serving it to its best advantage. Before serving any particular wine, make sure that it is adequately matured. Wine is rather like fruit, it ripens slowly then stays ripe for a while before going bad. Wine matures relatively slowly and then stays mature for quite a long time, many years perhaps, and then slowly begins to deteriorate. The right time to drink it then is after it has become fully mature and before it begins to deteriorate. As has been said previously, each wine takes a different period of time to mature and so it is important to ensure that the wine you are about to drink is fully mature and in fact ready for drinking. It should, of course, be star bright and of good colour. It should have a clean fresh bouquet of adequate depth. It should taste smooth and round, free from sharpness or bitterness.

Having satisfied yourself that the wine is suitably mature then you must consider whether it is the right wine for the occasion. There is such an immensely varied number of wines that clearly there are different wines for different purposes suitable for every occasion. Some wines are so totally different from others, that clearly if one wine were suitable the other would be totally out of place.

Broadly speaking, one drinks wine before a meal, during a meal and after a meal, and, except for sparkling wine, wines suitable for these three different purposes are not usually interchangeable. Wine to be drunk before a meal is meant to stimulate the appetite and refresh the taste buds of the mouth. It should therefore be clean and fresh to the taste rather than strongly flavoured and cloying to the palate. Apricot, grapefruit and orange wines, if they are dry and well matured, quite often make very pleasant aperitifs.

Table wines of course may be either red or white or rosé, and those intended to be served with the dessert may be sweet. Those meant to be served with fish or meat should be dry and varied according to the precise food with which they are to be served. Light foods require light wine to balance them. Roast meat and richer foods require a heavier wine containing more tannin and more alcohol to bring out the best flavour. Since relatively large quantities of table wine are sometimes consumed with a meal, the alcohol content should never exceed 12 per cent.

Wines that follow a meal are usually of two kinds. Strong rich fruity wines, to be consumed in small quantities immediately after a meal, such as port or cream sherry. The other kind is wine that is usually served with light refreshments and is called a social wine. It is very popular with many amateur wine makers. It ranges from fairly dry to medium sweet and it can be either red, white or rosé. It varies between 11 per cent and 13 per cent alcohol, and its commercial counterpart is the wine served at cheese and wine parties. Social wine can be made from an infinite variety of ingredients and very often it is made from many different ingredients, but frequently it is just a blend of different kinds of wine.

Sparkling wines are best served before a meal or as a social wine. They always seem to have something very special about them and it seems a pity to the author to lose this speciality against a background of food. They stimulate conversation, especially about themselves, which is sometimes lost if one is also concentrating on eating a meal.

The variety therefore is great, and you must be careful to select the right wine for the particular purpose for which it is to be drunk.

It used to be thought that serving wine at the right temperature was a connoisseur's foible. Experience shows, however, that light, white and rosé wines taste crisper and fresher if slightly chilled before serving them. An hour in the refrigerator is usually long enough, and a few minutes in an ice bucket does just as well. Somewhere between 45 and 50°F. (8–10°C.) is usually quite cold enough to serve a white or rosé wine. Red wines on the other hand benefit by being served free from chill so that the harshness of the tannin is somewhat softened and ameliorated. Around 70°F., 21°C. is usually about right for all red wines. Sparkling wines need to be served a little colder than white wines to ensure that the bubbles of carbon dioxide escape from the wine slowly and steadily rather than with a gushing rush which quickly leaves the wine bereft and still. Wines that have to be served free from chill should be stood in a warm room for several hours so that the warmth can be absorbed gradually and without affecting the wine. It should not on any occasion be stood in hot water or on a hot stove.

It sometimes assists a red wine to achieve room temperature by carefully pouring it into a clean decanter an hour before serving it. This not only enables the wine to come into contact with the warmer air more readily, but enables the wine to breathe for a short while and to develop additional bouquet by oxidation in the decanter. Since the wine has been stored in a dark bottle, serving it at table from a decanter shows the red wine off very much better since its brilliance and hue can be the more readily discerned. A polished clean glass decanter is immeasurably preferable on a table than a dark green bottle.

Whilst it is not so important to decant white and rosé wines, since unlike red wines they do not often throw a deposit in the bottle, nevertheless their appearance is still improved and often their bouquet and flavour too, by serving them from a decanter rather than from the bottle.

Decanters must always be kept scrupulously clean, and should be washed out immediately after use. They should never be left with just a few drops of red wine in them or white wine for that matter, because although it seems smooth, the inside of the decanter is often a little rough especially under the magnification of a microscope. The colour in a wine tends to settle in the tiny pores in the glass and to cause discoloration which is often difficult to remove.

If you have a decanter that has become soiled it is best cleaned with a bleach and then very thoroughly rinsed in clean cold water on many occasions to ensure that all traces of the bleach has been removed. Older recipes for cleaning decanters involve the use of sand or shot but these only aggravate the roughness and make the decanter more ready to pick up stains in future. When a decanter has been thoroughly washed and rinsed it should be up-ended to drain quite dry and should then be stored in a glass cabinet with the stopper out.

Great care should be taken in decanting a wine that has a deposit in the punt of the bottle. The cork should be carefully removed and the neck of the bottle wiped with a clean cloth. The bottle should be held in one hand up to a good light. The decanter should be held in the other hand and the bottle slowly tilted so that the wine trickles down the side of the decanter and does not splash into the bottom. As the sediment nears the neck of the bottle, pouring should cease so that no sediment passes into the decanter. The stopper should always be placed in the decanter when wine is inside so that dust and bacteria do not enter into the wine. Smoked glass or coloured decanters should never be used, and cut-glass decanters are only suitable if the cutting is not too deep. Engraved glass decanters may be used providing the engraving is relatively light.

When the wine is safe in the decanter you should now select your glasses. Every glass in which wine is to be served should have a stem so that it is never necessary for the hand or fingers to come into contact with the bowl of the glass containing wine. Greasy fingers detract from the appearance of the wine in the glass and the warmth given off by the hand can effect the temperature of the wine. The stem should sit on a firm base and support the bowl which should be incurved at the top. The purpose of this shape is to ensure that the bouquet given off by the wine is retained to some extent in the glass so that it can be smelt and savoured to the full. A bowl which opens wider at the top of the glass encourages the bouquet to escape as does a bowl which has absolutely vertical sides. The bowl, stem and base should be of clear glass since colour in the bowl will vary the colour of the wine and colour in the stem and base will reflect and therefore change the colour of the wine as well. For preference the bowl should be of clear plain glass free from cutting, engraving or painting. A glass is to wine what a frame is to a picture. It concentrates the gaze on the intended object without let or hindrance. The glass should be large enough to contain sufficient wine for the purpose when never more than half to two-thirds full. This enables the bowl to be moved in a circular manner so as to cause the wine to swirl in the glass, thus releasing its bouquet and allowing the folds of glycerine in the wine slowly to slip down the glass.

From the number of badly designed and coloured glasses on the market it would seem that very few people are conscious of the need to enjoy the appearance of the wine they are about to drink.

They miss a very great deal and have clearly got their priorities wrong. It is the wine which is important not the glass.

When pouring wine from a decanter care should be taken not to put too much wine into the glass. For some reason wine looks very much better in a glass that is not full. Furthermore it enables the bouquet to gather on top of the wine so that you can get your nose well into the bowl and inhale all the delightful aroma that is being released. Equally important, however, is the fact that one can safely move a glass that is only half to two-thirds full without spilling any on the tablecloth or one's clothes. There is something of an optical illusion here because one may have two or even three glasses of wine, each only half full, and one is under the impression that one is having a good deal to drink. On the other hand because the glasses are only half full the effect on one's person is not so dramatic as to cause one not to be able to enjoy drinking a further glass.

If you are serving wine from a tray there is no doubt that it looks best on a silver salver. In the absence of silver, however, mirrored steel does very well. If neither is available, a clean white table napkin covering any old tray is the next best thing. The silver, steel or white table napkin reflects the colour of the wine and shows it off to its best advantage without detracting from it in any way at all. Fancy trays on the other hand like fancy glasses, diminish the appearance of the wine and certainly distract one's attention from it.

After use, glasses should be washed in warm soapy water to remove the grease of finger marks outside and glycerine inside, and then rinsed in clean cold water upended and drained dry. The glasses should be polished and put away in a cupboard free from smell of stain, polish, varnish or any other odour which may taint the glass and subsequently the wine. Before use, the glass should always be freshly polished with a clean dry cloth so that it sparkles and looks inviting to the wine.

But few wines are meant to be drunk alone and nearly all wines taste very much better if served with suitable food. Some remarks have already been made on this subject but here it should be stated that palates vary enormously and that a wine enjoyed by one person with a particular dish is nausea to another. For example many people unaccustomed to wine prefer a sweet white wine with everything, whether it be roast beef, roast chicken, fish or sweet.

Others prefer a much drier wine with their main meal, since the acidity and tannin help to balance the fats and proteins. It is a truism to say that the more you know and learn about wine the better you enjoy it, and many people who start with a sweet palate steadily progress to one that enjoys very dry wines and finally reacts slightly, moving away just a fraction from the extremely dry.

The long established guide line of drinking red wine with red meat and white wine with white meat and fish has much to commend it. Considerable pleasure can be obtained from searching for the right food to accompany different wines, or, vice versa, the right wines to accompany different foods. Rosé wines graciously accompany most foods although cheese is generally at its best with a good red wine, whether dry or sweet and strong.

Before tasting wine it is always worthwhile to prepare one's taste buds with a mouthful of food; this provides a background against which the wine can be judged. The wine is meant to compliment the food and the one to balance the other.

With so much wine about the house, opportunities should be taken to use wine in the preparation of food. Wine made at home may be used in exactly the same way as wine bought from the wine merchant. The advantage is that because you have so much you can afford to experiment more readily than if you were spending £1 a bottle on your wine. Different wines accompany different parts of the meal and if you are planning to serve several courses you should aim to serve several different wines of different types. This is a great challenge to the winemaker and provides immense satisfaction if you are successful in blending together three or four different wines with different courses.

However lovely the wine and food, it is no use unless you have the right company with which to enjoy it. There are some people in the world who enjoy beer better than anything else, others prefer tea at all times. There are others who take but a tiny sip of wine and make such a fuss that you would think they had drunk the whole bottle! If you are having a little dinner party at which you propose to serve your own wines it is best to give some thought to the palates of your guests and if possible try to serve them the kind of wines that you think they will enjoy, and if you are in any doubt, serve them only very tiny portions at first. If they like what you have made you can always give them more. If

they don't you have not offended them and caused an embarrassment, nor have you wasted your wine. If you have gone to a lot of
trouble to serve your best wines, then make sure that your guests
are wine drinkers too and will really enjoy what you serve to them.
The right company can greatly enhance the pleasure given by the
wine and in turn the wine will enhance the pleasure given by your
guests.

Try to prepare sufficient wines for your needs for the evening,
but should they run out try not to serve an inferior wine or one
that has not been adequately prepared. One should always try to
finish on a high note as it were, and it is far better for you and
your guests to wish there was more of that lovely wine than to feel
that the last glass wasn't up to the rest and what a pity the evening
has been somewhat spoiled. If you finish your wines for the evening
when everyone is still clamouring for more, then you will make a
date for a future pleasure together. If you become satiated with a
wine not so good as your best there won't be much point in having
another evening, if it is going to finish in the same way.

When actually drinking the wine make sure that you get the very
most from it. First by holding your glass of wine to the light so
that you can enjoy its clarity and hue, and comment on its
brilliance and subtle colouring. Enjoy while you can the great
pleasures from the gift of sight. Then holding the base of the glass
between your finger and thumb, being careful not to touch the
bowl, having lifted the glass from the tray by its stem, move the
glass slowly to and fro beneath your nose. This will enable you to
appreciate the first vinous qualities of the bouquet before swirling
the wine to realease its aroma and further esters. This is the time to
get your nose well into the bowl and to inhale the bouquet as
deeply as you can, just as if you were smelling a lovely rose or some
other flower. There is room for further comment and appreciation
here before proceeding any further and there is no reason at all
why the act should not be repeated several times to make quite
sure that you have savoured both sight and smell to the full.

Next take a fair mouthful of wine slowly through the lips carefully noting its greeting, slowly allowing it to pass over the tongue
and around the gums and mouth. Pause while you appreciate its
smoothness, its good balance, texture and flavour. Chew it slowly,
protrude the tongue slightly and inhale slowly so that you can
further savour the bouquet from the reverse end of your olfactory

nerves as it were. Then slowly swallow the wine and continue to swallow several times until the farewell can be tasted at the very base of the tongue, reminding you of all the joys you have had in this particular wine and of others still to come. This is a moment for silence and deep appreciation. For the connoisseur it is a moment of analysis, documenting and noting in the memory for comparison on other occasions. This is the moment of truth and must not be hurried or lightly passed over. When all has been enjoyed, noted and remembered, it is time to resume conversation about the wine and to discuss various splendid and fine points with your guests. The enjoyment lingers on even in conversation.

There are few more satisfying pleasures in this world than to enjoy one of your own wines to the full in this manner. This great pleasure is spoiled, or at least diminished, if you have a bad cold or catarrh, if you have burnt your tongue on hot soup, if you have washed your hands in highly scented soap, or you are close to a person wearing a highly scented perfume. You need to be in good form to enjoy wine to the utmost in this manner. On the other hand you can drink wine at almost any time in your life. Young babies can have just a sip of wine and water from three or four months old. Children, consequently inquisitive, may safely enjoy wine in very small quantities. As they grow up it will have no mysteries for them and the desire to drink to excess will never tempt them. In convalescence from illness wine can be a tonic and to others a sedative. Even when spirits and beer are forbidden for health reasons, a dry table wine is always permitted. From the cradle to the grave wine can safely be one's constant companion to be enjoyed in moderation at all times. Home-made wine has the additional advantage of costing so little.

CHAPTER ELEVEN

The story of winemaking

Although it is not strictly necessary to know how wine was made in other ages, the story of winemaking is a fascinating one. Some knowledge of how wine was made in other days helps us better to understand the problems involved and so to make better wine today. The whole purpose of this chapter then is to provide additional background and from this background will be gained better understanding of winemaking today.

Many people are inclined to say that winemaking must be difficult and messy. But when one remembers that wine has been made for something like ten thousand years and that the facilities available in the past must have been primitive in the extreme, one can readily realise that winemaking is not really difficult or messy today at all. Wine has been traditionally made from grapes, no doubt because of the high juice content of the berry. The grape vine may very well have been one of the earliest plants to have been cultivated by man, perhaps as long ago as 6,000 years before the birth of Christ. In the famous Tigris/Euphrates area there is reason to believe that viticulture was well established long before 4,000 B.C.

We have clear evidence that the vine was cultivated and wine was made in Egypt 3,000 years before Christ and slowly spread into Crete and Southern Greece, then on to Italy and finally to the Marseilles area of France about 500 B.C. The Romans decreed laws about the planting of vines while they were in occupation of France, or Gaul as it was then known. Herodotus the famous Greek Historian, writing some 450 years B.C. not only recorded the making of wine casks from palm tree wood but also the making of wine from the fruit of the palm i.e. dates. Presumably lemons or some other citrus fruit was also added as otherwise it is difficult to see how any yeast could ferment such a must.

There are of course numerous references to wine in the Bible both before the birth of Christ and afterwards. It is clear that wine libations were poured in honour of heathen gods, notably the Greek Dionysis and later his Roman successor Bacchus. The Semitic tribes adopted this heathen habit and used wine and bread symbolically on the Sabbath eve. It was natural then for Christ, who was of course a Jew, to continue to use wine to represent his blood in the Sacrament.

Around the Mediterranean coast the wine that was made was no doubt sweet and strong, certainly more so than that made in the more northerly areas where lack of sunshine is likely to have made the wine slightly acid, thin and weaker.

Thick amphore were used in which to store wine and the point at which they ended was stuck in the soft sand to help hold them upright. The jars were usually sealed with beeswax or animal fat to keep out dirt and infection, especially that carried by flies. The winemakers then put their wine to mature in a cool dark place free from vibration and offering facilities for the sediment to deposit in the base of the jar.

The characteristics of these different wines was well known. We are told for example by Athenius when writing about A.D. 200 that a certain wine 'drives men out of their senses and makes women inclined to pregnancy'. Wine has long been thought to have aphrodisiacal qualities and since, when drunk in moderate quantities it releases one's inhibitions, the long held belief may well be true. Athenius also tells us that at about this time Celts, who we now know to have been living in the southern half of England, imported wine from Marseilles to be drunk by the merchants and perhaps the Court, whilst the working classes, so to speak, drank beer made from wheat and prepared with honey.

By the time Henry II married Eleanor of Aquitaine in the twelfth century, wine had been imported from France into England for more than 1,000 years. Nevertheless since Eleanor brought with her as a dowry the land of Aquitaine, the chief port of which was Bordeaux, there was an immediate and substantial increase in the quantities of wine brought into England from other parts of France. It must be remembered that English soldiers were stationed there and no doubt they were supported by a good deal of English trade. It seems only natural that wine should be shipped

Removing elderberries from their stalks. All green stems must be excluded

Preparing a yeast starter bottle. See how to crush hard tablets and note the cotton wool for plugging

back to pay for the armies and their needs. The Bordeaux region had been a splendid wine producing area for about 1,000 years and so viticulture and viniculture were well established. Two main kinds of wine were made, red and white, the white was rather sweet and full bodied, perhaps not dissimilar from the Sauterne so popular in this country today. The other was red, rather dry and somewhat harsh because of the great amount of tannin contained in the grapes skin and stalks, as well as the pips, all of which were macerated in the wine, which was then as now fermented on the pulp. The English soldiers, with their rather unsophisticated palates, found this red wine a bit too harsh for their liking, but on the other hand the white wine was really a little too sweet and cloying. Accordingly the wines were blended for the soldiers, and in ameliorating the flavour of the red wine and white wine also lightened its colour somewhat and so the wine was called Clairet, meaning clear or transparent. The word has remained in common use, reaching its peak in the nineteenth century as the word Claret, a generic title for all red wines imported from the Bordeaux area. Blending no longer continues of course but the name has remained.

During this time ale was still being made in England and slowly nettle flavouring was being replaced by hop flavouring, although the hops at that time were still being imported from the Continent. Soon, however, the Kent hop fields were established and by the fourteenth century all the ale being brewed was flavoured with hops.

Over in the West Country, in Herefordshire in particular and also in Somersetshire, cider orchards were being developed and the craft of making cider was constantly being improved. By the middle of the seventeenth century, i.e., about 1670, cider enjoyed its Golden Age. Writers tell us that the best English cider was often considerably superior to imported French wine. Methods of making cider were fully described with illustrations of the press used, and details of the special apples that were used were also given. Fundamentally cider making hasn't changed since that time although it went into a great decline for a while and is only now beginning to climb back into popularity. Better varieties of apples have more recently been developed, but some commercial cider makers still used old fashioned methods and fail to use adequate sulphite in the preparation of the must. As a result the apples oxidise and the

F

flavour is carried through in to the finished cider.

In the sixteenth and seventeenth centuries, the most common ailment of the day was stone of the bladder and the physicians of the period thought that this was caused by drinking too much red wine which tended to overheat the body and therefore cause the hard minerals to coalesce to form a stone. They advocated the drinking of white wine from Germany, where it was grown along the banks of the River Rhine. This was thought to have a cooling effect and to be more beneficial. Wine was frequently used as a medicine in itself and was given to a person suffering from shock or a wound, and indeed wounds were often washed in wine to cleanse them. Sometimes herbs, spices and other medicaments were dissolved in the wine and given to patients to drink to relieve them from their sufferings. This ancient habit is of course still in use and there are many tonic wines on the market claiming to speed convalescence and recovery.

Mead of course was commonly made throughout the country. All the great houses, farms and monasteries had a room given over to the making of fermented drinks. It was called the Still Room. not because it contained a still with which to distill wine into spirits but rather because the room was kept clean, cool and calm so that the ales, meads and wines could ferment and mature in the best possible conditions available. Winemaking at home in the sense as we now understand it, i.e., the making of wines from different fruits, flowers and vegetables as opposed to the exclusive use of grapes, developed towards the end of the seventeenth century and by the eighteenth century the making of fruit wine was encouraged by countless books of recipes. Not until 1816 was any serious study of wine making published and wines that were made were undoubtedly lacking in alcohol and were terribly sweet. This was no doubt due to the fact that they frequently contained far too little acid, always contained too much sugar and probably insufficient yeast of the right kind as well. However, by the eighteenth century some good English wines were being made and were often used by wine merchants to improve the imported Continental wines which had suffered in their journey from their home vineyard. Gooseberry, cherry and elderberry wines were especially used for blending purposes and of course the resultant wine was sold as a superior imported wine rather than a blend of English and foreign wines.

Modern winemakers have learned much from this trick of the trade and nowadays grape juice concentrate is very frequently added to English musts to improve the vinosity and quality of our English wines.

The importance of racking wine, i.e., siphoning the clear wine from the sediment in the bottom of a bottle or jar was known and understood and frequently practiced. Indeed, it was regarded as the panacea for all ills. The need for hygiene was appreciated and sometimes sulphur was burned in a cask to purify it. The importance of keeping the bung hole covered by a pebble stone during fermentation was learned by some and not by others. Modern winemakers have adopted this lesson into the use of the current fermentation lock, which keeps dust, dirt and bacteria out of the wine yet enables the carbon dioxide gas to escape freely and without difficulty.

Most wines were left to ferment with the wild yeast on the skins of the fruit and this may account for the low alcoholic content of the wine, since this particular strain of yeast *Saccharomyces apiculati*, has a very low alcoholic tolerance of little more than 4 per cent.

Indicative of the state of knowledge of yeasts in 1814 is this quotation from a book written by a man named Cushing, 'Vinous fermentation may be said to be a divine operation which the omniscient Creator has placed in our cup of life, to transmute the fruits of the earth into wine for the benefit and comfort of his creatures.' So fermentation was thought to be a divine operation and obviously a good number of poor quality wines must have been made.

Spirit, notably Brandy, was very cheap, and nearly all recipes recommended the mixture of Brandy with the finished wine. In spite of the shortcomings of the wine made in the eighteenth and nineteenth centuries, clearly enough of it must have been good enough to make it well worthwhile continuing to make it. Indeed, Jane Austen was reported to have been a dab hand at making orange and gooseberry wines which were said to have been of a very high quality indeed. If she had taken the trouble to have read the better books which by then had been published, it could well be that she knew almost as much about winemaking as we do today and could very well have had the same excellent results. By the early nineteenth century, winemaking at home was very well and widely established and there is a reference in the book, *The British Winemaker*, which was published in 1835 to the 'Amateur Winemaker'. The author, a man named W. H. Roberts, who was a brewer by trade recommended the use of the hydrometer for checking the specific gravity of the juice and then of the must after the sugar had been added, and of the wine during fermentation and at its close.

Unfortunately Mrs Beaton who shortly after collected together countless recipes, frequently got hold of the wrong ones, and very few of the recipes that she recommended were likely to have made very good wines. Certainly not for the sophisticated palate. Clearly Mrs Beaton knew nothing about the principles of making wine and had probably not read any of the splendid books that had then been published and which had sold surprisingly well considering the limitations on distribution in those days.

As the industrial urbanisation reached its climax towards the end of the nineteenth century and countless terraced cottages were built back to back in congested towns, the *ancient* craft of winemaking with all its cultured and civilising benefits fell into a decline. Its place was taken by gin with its devastating and deadening effects on humanity, and by the cup of tea which England has made famous.

In 1945, however, after the people of Great Britain had twice teetered on the brink of disaster in two cataclysmic wars, reaction set in and people started to make wine again. Surburbia, garden cities and developing villages, now contain the homes where wine is made year by year. What was at first something of a joke among the cranks has become respectable and popular.

The development of scientific knowledge during the last sixty years in particular, and a full understanding of the use of yeast, or rather the part played by yeast in fermentation, together with the need for acids and nutrients, and perhaps above all else the urgent and important use of sulphite both in the preparation of the must and in hygiene throughout winemaking, enables good sound wine to be made every time without failure. The increasing cost of living coupled with visits to the Continent where wine is freely drunk, brought home to many people the need to make and enjoy their own wines.

Winemaking in England is probably in its 'Golden Age' at the moment and at the time of writing, expansion and improvement continues. If you follow the practices recommended in this book you cannot help but make excellent wine which you will thoroughly enjoy. It will add to your life a state of gracious living and in your turn you will be able to pass on your knowledge and experience of a civilised way of life to your children and your children's children.

CHAPTER TWELVE

The Fellowship of Winemakers and Brewers

If ever you have been to a floral or horticultural show or to one of the County or Borough Shows held annually in every part of the country it is probable that you have seen a display of home-made wines, beers and meads. Not only in Great Britain but also in many parts of the world, there are now Associations of Winemakers who meet regularly to discuss methods of improving their standard of winemaking, comparing the wines they make with the wines made by their fellow club members. This is perhaps one of the most effective means of increasing one's knowledge of winemaking, and the extremely sociable nature of the people making wine add pleasure to the learning. These winemakers and many others not members of clubs, enter their wines in the local County Shows. The wines are appraised by skilled judges who have to pass a rigorous examination before they are admitted to the Amateur Wine Makers' National Guild of Judges.

Whilst there is a fairly wide range of quality in the wines submitted, there is no doubt that the best are extremely good indeed and compare most favourably with good wines anywhere. It is a most worthwhile exercise to prepare several bottles of wine for such a show and to receive the appraisal of an impartial expert. If your wine is awarded a place, your head may feel too large even for a crown of glory. If it is not awarded a place you will find the comments and advice of the judge most helpful and you will be determined next year to do much better.

The National Guild of Judges was formed in the Autumn of 1963 after almost a year of negotiation and discussion largely prompted and stimulated by the author and Mr S. W. Andrews of Hertford. Mr Andrews became the Founder Chairman and the author became the first Secretary of the Guild. Together with a small committee they produced a handbook for the guidance of judges, exhibitors and show organisers. The standards outlined therein were unanimously adopted by every member of the Guild and are now the nationally accepted standards for judging wine and beer made at home. Examination systems were immediately set up and there has been a constant demand from candidates wishing to take the examination to become members of the Guild.

The examination begins with a rigorous practical examination that can take three to four hours. The candidate has to taste each wine in a given class and express his or her comments to an adjudicator, just as if the candidate were conducting the adjudication of the wine alone. This extends to placing the best wines in the order in which the candidate thinks they should be placed. The results are then compared with the official examiner's adjudication. The pass mark is extremely high but the ordeal is not yet over. The practical examination is followed by two oral examinations, one on the theory of judging and knowledge of the Guild handbook and the other on the theory of winemaking. Only about a third of the candidates are successful but each year there are a number of new entrants to the Guild and so the membership is increasing steadily. The advantage of the Guild and the rigorous examination means that exhibitors in shows judged by members of the National Guild of Judges can be assured of an objective appraisal of their wine by someone with considerable knowledge and experience both of winemaking and of adjudication. Each judge fills in a standard marking sheet for each bottle of wine appraised, and awards marks up to the maximum set out below :

Presentation	2
Clarity and colour	4
Bouquet	4
Flavour and quality	20
Total	30

The reasons for awarding or deducting marks are clearly set out in the *Guild Handbook* and so each judge follows precisely the same system. As far as is humanly possible, objective appraisal takes the place of subjective appreciation.

Before you enter your wine in a show you should obtain a copy of the show schedule and study carefully the regulations covering the wine section. Memorise the different classes and make a note of those classes for which you have bottles of wine suitable for entry. Send in your application in good time to the show secretary and then begin to prepare your wines.

Start by selecting your best clear-glass wine bottles, free from scratches, chips and blemishes. Wash them thoroughly both inside and out using a bottle brush internally. Rinse the bottles carefully in cold water several times and up-end them to drain until dry.

In the same manner select sufficient of your very best all cork flange stoppers. These are T-shaped corks and not cylindrical storage corks. These corks have been chosen so that they can be removed easily when the judge is appraising the wine and can just as easily be returned to the bottles. If cylindrical corks were used, corkscrews would have to be used to withdraw the corks, which might well break up, would be difficult to re-insert in the bottles and in any case would look ragged and jagged when the exhibition was opened to the public. The cork stoppers ensure a neatly finished appearance together with ease in use. No cork that is mouldly, soiled or dirty should ever be used. The new corks should be thoroughly washed in a Campden tablet solution to ensure that they are clean and sterile, free from chalk, dust and other impurities.

It is absolutely imperative to ensure that the finished bottle of wine to be entered in the show should contain no trace of any sediment or portion of cork, or any other impurity of any kind. To this end many exhibitors take the top half of two bottles of the same wine and pour them carefully into the prepared exhibition bottle. The bottle should be filled to within half to three-quarters of an inch of the bottom of the cork stopper when inserted in the bottle. The corks should be fitted tightly into the bottles, and the labels which have been received from the show secretary should be affixed in the places prescribed. This is usually 1 in. from the bottom of the bottle (not the bottom of the punt). This means at the show that all the labels will be evenly placed – again giving a neat and orderly appearance to the bottles.

Examination of the bottles will reveal two seams since most bottles are moulded and joined together. Great care should be taken to ensure that the labels are stuck between the seams and never closer to one than the other or worse still across a seam. This would give a poor appearance to the finish of the bottle and would lose marks.

Finally, the bottle should be wiped over with a clean teatowel to ensure that no finger marks or traces of gum appear on the bottle in any place. At this stage many exhibitors then wrap their bottles in tissue paper to keep them in first class condition until the show.

Before taking your bottles along to the stewards at the show at the time mentioned in the regulations, just check carefully that you have entered the right wines in the right classes. At every show one or two people manage to put a red wine into a white class or vice versa, or more commonly a sweet wine into a dry class or a dry wine into a sweet class. Dryness is often equated with acidity in the minds of inexperienced exhibitors and for this reason it is very useful to check the specific gravity of your wines with an hydrometer shortly before entering them. Wines in a dry class should certainly not exceed a specific gravity of 1.000 and wines in the sweet class should certainly have a specific gravity of at least 1.010. To make a mistake in entering a wine in the wrong class, is the kind of mistake for which you could willingly kick yourself. Unfortunately your bottle will be marked 'NAS' meaning not according to schedule, and will not be appraised by the judge. This is a very simple check and one that should not be ignored or overlooked.

If you have several wines suitable for entry into a particular class and you are in doubt which wine to enter, then you should have a little judging session by yourself with your own wines before making up your mind. First prepare a clean glass for each wine and a little cheese or plain biscuits with which to cleanse your palate after tasting each one. Then inspect each bottle of wine for clarity and colour, looking for brilliance in the clarity, for the judge will be seeking a star bright wine; one that has the least haze or lack of brightness will certainly lose marks. Together with perfect clarity should go a splendid colour. White wines should have a hint of gold about them so that they can be seen and admired. Wines that are so pale that they look like water generally lose marks. Except in appropriate classes, brown and tawny coloured wines show up poorly against those of better hue. Red wines should be a good rich red without hints of brown, blue or black. When held to the light it should really please the eye and possess what is known as a fine 'robe'. Award each of your bottles of wine up to four points for their appearance in clarity and colour.

Taking one wine at a time now pour a little into each glass and stand the glass in front of the bottle so that there is no misunderstanding from which bottle the given wine came. Then in turn inhale the bouquet from each wine and compare one with another. The judge will deduct marks for lack of vinosity, lack of depth in bouquet, for any unwelcome smells that are off-putting or reminiscent of vinegar or acidity, excessive sweetness or excessive alcohol. The judge will be looking for a wine with a good clean bouquet that is attractive to smell, and that there is enough bouquet there to smell and savour. Award each wine up to four points for its bouquet.

Next take the wines one at a time, lift them to your mouth and imbibe a good mouthful noting your first reaction as it greets your lips, tongue and gums. Chew the wine slowly in your mouth and if possible open your lips slightly, push out your tongue slightly and try to inhale a little air through your mouth. This will bring out all the very best in the flavour and taste of the wine. Excessive acidity will be registered on the tip of the tongue. Excessive tannin and bitterness will be noticed on both sides of the tongue towards the back. Sweetness is noted on the top flat part of the tongue and alcohol on the back of the tongue.

After a few moments spit out the wine and swallow several times so that you can taste the 'farewell' at the very base of the tongue. This is the most searching test for any wine and if it does possess any faults at all they will certainly show up here. On the other hand its virtues show up equally well and there is great pleasure to be enjoyed from savouring a splendid 'farewell'. After ruminating in your mind for some moments about what you have experienced, award the wine up to 20 marks for balance, flavour and quality.

Do this with each wine, then add up the marks. Clearly you enter the one with the highest marks. You may have learned a good deal about your own wine in the process. If you ever get the chance never miss the opportunity of acting as a steward to a judge and with any luck he will allow you to taste each of the wines he is appraising. In two hours or so you may be able to taste upwards of forty wines. In this wide range of experience you will certainly find some extremely lovely wines, a fair number of average, day to day, run of the mill wines, with no particular faults but just lacking that character, breeding and finesse that makes a good wine stand out from an average wine. You will probably also find one or two wines which have quite noticeable faults and from which you can learn a useful and valuable lesson.

If there is a Winemaking Association in your neighbourhood it will be well worth your while to join if you can gain admittance and in a few years you will find the standards of your winemaking improve enormously. Most clubs meet once a month under the chairmanship of one of the more experienced members. Guest speakers are invited to come and talk on different topics and aspects of winemaking, beer brewing, mead making and preparing wines for exhibition and comparative appraisal of other wines. Sometimes commercial wines are bought for comparison and the results are frequently most revealing. Our home-made wines frequently compare extremely well indeed. Each Association, Club, Guild or Circle, (they often have any or none of these names) varies widely in the atmosphere they engender and the work they undertake. Club evenings are most convivial occasions and you are sure to find someone there with other interests similar to your own. Mostly they are mixed clubs usually consisting of husband and wife though there are individual members of either sexes. Many clubs hold their own internal competition once a year, this might very well be regarded as the 'Nursery Stakes' prior to entering into regional shows and perhaps later on the great National Show which is held once a year. At the National Show upwards of 3,000 bottles are entered for adjudication by 60 or more judges and usually more than 1,000 members turn up to see the show and to listen to the lectures.

Clubs usually have a supplies officer who buys many ingredients in bulk for re-sale to the members. This is a tremendous chore for the supplies officer but a great boon and benefit to the ordinary member.

Whilst most of the emphasis in this chapter has been on wine, beer and mead classes are also available in competitions. The standards here are also extremely high.

Beer has to be presented in a screw-stoppered beer bottle which must be as clean as the wine bottle already mentioned. The bottle should contain as little deposit as possible although it is essential that when the beer is poured it should have a good head and be able to retain its lively condition for some while in the glass. It should of course also be star bright and free from any haze. It should be of excellent flavour within its class, whether light ale, brown ale or stout.

Pure meads and fruit meads are judged to the same high standard. Dry mead should contain little if any reminiscence of honey from which it is made, though a little taste of honey is expected in the sweet meads.

There is much satisfaction in being able to make wines, beers and meads up to prize winning standards. Even if you are not a 'pot hunter' there are countless trophies awarded for the best wines in special classes or the most number of points gained in a group of classes. There are always a few members who are anxious to win these trophies year after year. These member take great pains to produce excellent wines in superb presentation and often deserve to win. Even so the difference between the first six wines at the show is often very slight indeed and to get any placing is an acknowledgement that you have made a jolly good wine.

When adjudicating at shows the author has frequently said to an exhibitor if his wine was of a particularly high standard, even if it had not won a first prize that it was a wine of which the exhibitor could well be proud and the adjudicator would be pleased to drink every day. Once you have achieved winemaking to this standard you can be sure that your wine is as good as the best that is made.

The handbook of the Amateur Wine Maker's National Guild of Judges costs 25p and is available not only from the Guild, but also from the Editor of *The Amateur Wine Maker*, North Croye, Croye Drive, The Avenue, Andover, Hampshire. It is also available in most public libraries for inspection.

After you have made wine for a year or two you will have sufficient wines from which to choose. It is very well worthwhile entering in the local show just to see how you are getting on. At nearly all shows the person who has judged a particular class is available to answer questions from the exhibitor about the wine that has been appraised. Never fail to take advantage of this opportunity to learn as much as you can from other people's opinions and experience.

CHAPTER THIRTEEN

Recipes for all occasions

I APÉRITIFS–RED, ROSÉ AND WHITE

It is not easy to make a good apéritif wine. It needs to be exceptionally well-balanced between flavour, body and alcohol, acid, tannin and sugar content. A dry sherry is the best known example, but dry white port can be delicious too. The choice of the most suitable ingredients is somewhat limited, but the following recipes have all given good results and are well worth making. Really adequate maturity is essential and two years may be necessary for some of these wines to reach their peak.

PINEAPPLE AND GRAPEFRUIT
Ingredients
4 fresh pineapples
4 grapefruit
1 lb sultanas
3 lb sugar
1 gallon water
German yeast – Liebfraumilch, Hock or the like
nutrient tablet
Campden tablets
Pectolase

Method
1 Top and tail the pineapples, but do not peel them. Cut them into small chunks and place them in a mashing vessel.
2 Halve the grapefruits, squeeze out all the juice and add to the pineapple.
3 Wash and cut the sultanas and add to the rest of the fruit.
4 Pour on 1 gallon of cold water and add 1 teaspoonful of

Pectolase and 1 crushed Campden tablet.

5 Cover the vessel and leave for 24 hours in a warm place.

6 Stir in 1 lb sugar, the nutrient and active yeast.

7 Ferment for 4–6 days, then strain off the solids.

8 Stir in the rest of the sugar and continue the fermentation in a jar fitted with an air lock.

9 When fermentation is finished rack into a clean storage jar and add another crushed Campden tablet.

10 When the wine is clear, rack again and store for six to nine months. Then bottle and leave for a further six months.

WHITE KNIGHT

Ingredients

3 lb fresh apricots
1 lb bananas
1 lemon and 1 grapefruit
1 lb seedless grapes
1 lb greengages
1 gallon water
3 lb sugar
Chablis yeast
Campden tablets
Pectolase
Nutrient

Method

1 Wash, quarter and stone the apricots and the greengages.

2 Peel the bananas and crush them.

3 Thinly pare the lemon and squeeze out the juice of both the lemon and the grapefruit.

4 Wash and crush the grapes, discarding the main stalk.

5 Put all the fruit, lemon rind and the juices into a mashing vessel and pour on 1 gallon of cold water. Add 1 teaspoonful of Pectolase and 1 crushed Campden tablet, then cover and leave for twenty-four hours.

7 Stir in 1 lb of sugar, the nutrient and the active yeast.

8 Ferment on the pulp for 4 or 5 days then strain off the solids and stir in 2 lb sugar.

9 Pour the must into a fermentation jar, fit an air lock and leave in a warm place until fermentation finishes.

10 When the wine begins to clear, rack into a clean storage jar,

add 1 crushed Campden tablet and store for 4 weeks.

11 When the wine is clear, rack again and store for six to nine months, then bottle and store for at least another six months.

ESPANA

Ingredients

3 lb Seville oranges
2 lb sweet oranges
2 lb bananas
1 lb apples
1 lb sultanas
14 pints cold water
6 lb sugar
Sherry yeast
Nutrient
Campden tablets
Pectolase
1 teaspoonful tannin

Method

1 Pour the water into a mashing vessel and sprinkle on two crushed Campden tablets.

2 Wash the oranges and thinly pare only the Sevilles dropping the peel into the water.

3 Halve all the oranges, squeeze out the juice and add to the water.

4 Peel and crush the bananas and add to the water. The skins should be discarded.

5 Wash the apples and crush finely or cut into small pieces and add to the water.

6 Chop up the sultanas and add to the rest of the fruit.

7 Add 2 teaspoonfuls of Pectolase.

8 Cover the vessel and leave it in a warm place for forty-eight hours.

9 Prepare a Sherry yeast in a starter bottle and when active add it to the must together with 1 level teaspoonful of tannin and 2 nutrient tablets.

10 Ferment on the pulp for 5 days and then strain out the solids.

11 Stir in 4 lb sugar and continue fermentation under an air lock, but with some head room.

12 One week later take out a quantity of wine, dissolve 1 lb

sugar in it and pour it back into the bulk.

13 A further week later repeat the process.

14 If the wine is dry when fermentation slows down repeat the process with ½ lb sugar.

15 When the wine begins to clear rack it off into a clean jar leaving a little headroom for air and add 2 crushed Campden tablets.

16 As soon as the wine is bright rack it again still leaving the head room for air and store at 60°F. until at least the following January.

17 Bottle and store at 55°F. for at least another six months, preferably twelve.

18 Serve chilled with various canapé.

ROSANA
Ingredients
8 oz dried rosehip shells
8 oz dried bananas
8 oz sultanas
4 oz dried figs
Rind and juice of 2 lemons
3 lb sugar
1 gallon hot water
Campden tablet
Pectolase
Nutrient
Tannin
Sherry yeast

Method
1 Wash the rosehip shells free of dust and place them in a mashing vessel.

2 Chop the bananas, sultanas and figs and add to the rosehips.

3 Pour on 8 pints of boiling water, cover the vessel and leave it to cool.

4 Add 1 crushed Campden tablet, 1 teaspoonful Pectolase, ¼ teaspoonful grape tannin, re-cover the vessel and leave it for forty-eight hours.

5 Prepare a Sherry yeast starter and when active add it to the must together with the nutrient.

6 Ferment on the pulp for 5 days, then strain out the solids and stir in 2 lb sugar.

Preparing to use a corker. Note that the corks have been soaking till they are soft

Finishing the appearance. Note the punted wine bottles, the flush fitting cork and foil as well as the fancy label

7 Fit an air lock and continue fermentation.

8 One week later remove some wine, dissolve the rest of the sugar and ferment to dryness.

9 Rack and mature as above.

PRUNE
Ingredients
4 lb best prunes
6 oz white grape juice concentrate
2 teaspoonfuls citric acid
$\frac{1}{2}$ teaspoonful grape tannin
2 teaspoonfuls Pectolase
$2\frac{1}{2}$–3 lb sugar
Water to 1 gallon
Sherry yeast
Campden tablets
Nutrient

Method
1 Wash the prunes, place them in a mashing vessel and pour six pints boiling water on them.

2 When cool mash the fruit and remove the stones.

3 Stir in 2 teaspoonsful Pectolase, 2 teaspoonsful citric acid, $\frac{1}{2}$ teaspoonful grape tannin and 1 crushed Campden tablet.

4 Cover and leave for 2 days, stirring twice daily.

5 Stir in the grape juice concentrate, nutrient and an active yeast.

6 Ferment on the pulp for 5 days then strain out the solids and stir in 2 lb sugar.

7 Fit an air lock and ferment in a warm place.

8 After one week stir in another $\frac{1}{2}$ lb sugar and continue fermentation.

9 If the specific gravity drops rapidly to 1.000 stir in another $\frac{1}{2}$ lb sugar. The aim is to ferment as much sugar as possible whilst keeping the specific gravity low since the wine should finish medium dry.

10 Rack and add 1 crushed Campden tablet and when the wine is clear rack again and store for one year. Bottle and keep for a further year if possible.

*   *   *

II TABLE WINES – RED, ROSÉ AND WHITE

As their name implies these wines are designed to be consumed with a meal. They should, therefore, not be too strong in alcohol : 10–12 per cent is ample. A great variety of ingredients may be used including flowers and vegetables but fruit wines tend to give the best results.

You will need to make rosé, white and red table wines to serve with different meals. The white and rosé wines should be served chilled at about 55°F. The red wines should be served at room temperature, about 67°F.

The red wines should be dry. The rosé wines not quite dry or just slightly sweet. The white wines should be either dry for serving with main courses or sweet for serving with desserts.

Many of these wines will keep several years, but in the main they are mature at about one year and may be drunk from then on.

RED WINES

BILBERRY WINE

These black berries grow on small shrubs about 18 in. high. Although they are not grown commercially in England the shrubs are now available from nurserymen for home cultivation. Dried, canned and bottled bilberries, sometimes know as whortleberries, are imported freely, however, and are readily available. They make an attractive wine and mix well with other fruits.

Ingredients
1 lb bottled or canned bilberries or ½ lb dried bilberries
6 oz black grape juice concentrate
2 lb sugar
1 teaspoonful Pectolase
¼ teaspoonful tannin
1 teaspoonful citric acid
Burgundy or Pommard yeast and nutrient
Water to 1 gallon

Method
1 Put the bilberries in a saucepan with 4 pints water, bring to the boil and simmer them gently for 5 minutes.

2 Pour them into a vessel and when cool stir in the grape juice concentrate, acid, tannin, Pectolase, a nutrient and active yeast.

3 Ferment for 4 days on the pulp then strain off the solids.

4 Stir in the sugar previously dissolved in 2 pints warm water and allow to cool.

5 Top up to 1 gallon with cold boiled water, fit an air lock and ferment to dryness.

6 Rack as a deposit forms and again when clear. Store for six months in jar and six months in bottle.

BLACKBERRY AND APPLE

Ingredients

3 lb ripe blackberries
4 lb mixed windfall apples
6 oz black grape juice concentrate
2½ lb sugar
Water to 1 gallon
Pectolase, Campden tablets
Pommard yeast and nutrient

Method

1 Crush 2 Campden tablets and dissolve them in 6 pints cold water together with 1 teaspoonful of Pectolase.

2 Wash and crush the apples including the cores and drop them into the water.

3 Wash and mash the blackberries and drop them into the water.

4 Cover the vessel and leave to stand for 2 days.

5 Stir in the grape juice concentrate, yeast and nutrient and then check the specific gravity of the must.

6 Ferment on the pulp for 5 days then strain out the solids.

7 Check the specific gravity and stir in sufficient sugar to bring the total specific gravity up to 1.085.

8 Fit an air lock and ferment to dryness.

9 Rack and store for one year, then bottle and keep for six months.

BLACKCURRANT AND BANANA WINE

Ingredients

2 lb blackcurrants
1 lb bananas
12 oz black grape juice concentrate
2 lb sugar

Water to 1 gallon
Pectolase and Campden tablet
Pommard yeast and nutrient

Method
1 Wash the blackcurrants and remove the main stalks.
2 Peel and mash the bananas.
3 Put the blackcurrants and bananas in a mashing vessel and pour
5 pints cold water over them.
4 Add 1 teaspoonful of Pectolase and 1 crushed Campden tablet.
Cover the vessel and leave for twenty-four hours.
5 Stir in the grape juice concentrate, the nutrient and an active
yeast.
6 Ferment on the pulp for 5 days then strain out the solids.
7 Stir in the sugar, fit an air lock and ferment to dryness.
8 Rack and store for one year, then bottle for six months.

ELDERBERRY AND APPLE WINE
Ingredients
1½ lb black ripe elderberries
4 lb windfall apples
1 lb bananas
6 oz black grape juice concentrate
2½ lb sugar
Water to 1 gallon
Pectolase
Pommard yeast and nutrient

Method
1 Stalk and wash the elderberries, peel and mash the bananas and
place them all in a saucepan, pour on 2 quarts water, bring to
the boil, simmer for 5 minutes then pour into a mashing vessel.
2 Wash and crush the apples and drop them into the must.
3 When cool stir in 1 teaspoonful Pectolase, the nutrient and an
active yeast.
4 Check and note the specific gravity.
5 After 5 days, strain off the solids, stir in the grape juice concentrate and check the specific gravity.
6 Add sufficient sugar to make a total specific gravity of 1.085.
7 Fit an air lock and ferment to dryness.
8 Rack and store for one year and then bottle for six months.

DAMSON AND PEAR

Ingredients
3 lb ripe damsons
3 lb hard pears
6 oz black grape juice concentrate
2¼ lb sugar
Water to 1 gallon
Pectolase
Bordeaux yeast and nutrient

Method
1 Stalk and wash the damsons place them in a mashing vessel and pour 6 pints boiling water over them.
2 When cool mash the fruit and remove the stones.
3 Wash and crush the pears and drop them into the must together with 1 teaspoonful Pectolase.
4 Stir in the grape juice concentrate, the nutrient and an active yeast.
5 Ferment on the pulp for 7 days then strain out the solids, stir in the sugar and fit an air lock.
6 Ferment to dryness then rack and store for six months. Bottle and keep for a further six months.

PLUM AND APPLE WINE

Ingredients
4 lb black cooking plums
4 lb windfall apples
6 oz black grape juice concentrate
2¼ lb sugar
Water to 1 gallon
Campden tablet
Pectolase
Pommard yeast and nutrient

Method
1 Wash the plums, pour 4 pints boiling water over them and leave them to cool.
2 Mash the plums with your hands to release the stones, take them out and throw them away.
3 Stir in 1 crushed Campden tablet and 1 teaspoonful Pectolase.

4 Wash and crush the apples, drop them into the must, cover and leave for twenty-four hours.

5 Next day stir in the nutrient, active yeast and grape juice concentrate.

6 Ferment on the pulp for 5 days then strain out the solids, stir in the sugar and top up with cold water to 8½ pints.

7 Ferment under an air lock to dryness then rack and store for six months, bottle and keep for a further six months.

ROSÉ WINES

CHERRY WINE

Ingredients

6 lb mixed cherries both red and white and including some cooking cherries

8 oz sultanas

2 lb sugar

Juice of 1 large lemon

¼ teaspoonful grape tannin

Water to 1 gallon

Pectolase

Campden tablets

Champagne yeast and nutrient

Method

1 Stalk and wash the cherries and pour 5 pints boiling water on to them. When cool mash them with you hands and remove the stones.

2 Wash and chop the sultanas, add them to the cherries and stir in 1 crushed Campden tablet, 1 teaspoonful Pectolase and the lemon juice. Cover and leave in a warm place for twenty-four hours.

3 Stir in the tannin, nutrient and active yeast and ferment on the pulp for 5 days.

4 Strain out the solids, stir in the sugar, fit an air lock and ferment to specific gravity 1.004.

5 Siphon into a clean jar and add 2 crushed Campden tablets.

6 Rack again when a deposit appears and again when the wine is clear.

7 Store for six months, then bottle and keep for a further six months.

REDCURRANT WINE
Ingredients
3 lb redcurrants
½ lb sultanas
2 lb sugar
Water to 1 gallon
Pectolase
Campden tablets
Champagne yeast and nutrient

Method
1 Wash the currants and remove only the main stalk. Crush them and place them in a vessel with 5 pints cold water.
2 Wash and chop the sultanas and add to the must.
3 Stir in 1 crushed Campden tablet and 1 teaspoonful Pectolase. Cover the vessel and leave for twenty-four hours.
4 Next day stir in the nutrient and an active yeast. Cover and ferment on the pulp for 4 days.
5 Strain out the solids, stir in the sugar, top up with cold boiled water if necessary and continue fermentation under an air lock.
6 Check the specific gravity from time to time and when it reaches specific gravity 1.004 rack into a clean jar and add two crushed Campden tablets.
7 Rack again as soon as a further deposit appears and again when clear.
8 Store for six months then bottle and keep for a further six months.
Note : The wine should taste slightly sweet and not dry.

ROSE PETAL WINE
Ingredients
2 quarts red rose petals from varieties such as Josephine Bruce, Fragrant Cloud, Madame Lapérière and the like
1 lb sultanas
Juice of 1 large lemon
2 lb sugar
¼ teaspoonful grape tannin
Water to 1 gallon
Champagne yeast and nutrient, Campden tablets

Method
1 Remove the petals from blown roses just before natural petal-

fall and pour 3 quarts warm water at about 120°F. over them. Cover the vessel and leave for twenty-four hours, but from time to time macerate them with a wooden spoon to extract the colour and perfume.

2 Wash and chop or mince the sultanas, place them in a vessel and pour the flower water over them.

3 Add the lemon juice, tannin, nutrient and active yeast and ferment for 7 days.

Note : If two quarts of rose petals are not available at one time, 1 quart may be used with 3 pints of water. A further quart of flowers and 3 pints of water may be prepared some days later and added to the sultanas.

4 Strain the sultanas, stir in the sugar, fit an air lock and ferment to specific gravity 1.004.

5 Siphon into a clean jar and stir in 2 crushed Campden tablets.

6 Rack again as soon as there is another deposit and again when the wine is clear.

7 Store for six months in jar, then bottle and keep for another six months.

STRAWBERRY JAM WINE

Ingredients

2 lb best quality strawberry jam
8 oz sultanas
1 lb sugar
Juice of 1 large lemon
6 pints water
Pectolase
¼ teaspoonful of grape tannin
Campden tablets
Champagne yeast and nutrient

Method

1 Wash and chop or mince the sultanas and place them in a mashing vessel.

2 Add the strawberry jam, the lemon juice, 2 teaspoonsful Pectolase (double the usual quantity) and 6 pints of tepid water (100°F.).

3 Stir gently till the jam is completely dissolved then add the tannin, nutrient and an active yeast.

4 Ferment for 7 days, then strain out the solids and stir in the

sugar. Make up to 1 gallon with cold boiled water if necessary.

5 Ferment under an air lock till the specific gravity reaches 1.004, then siphon into a clean jar and add 2 crushed Campden tablets.

6 Rack when a deposit appears and again when the wine is clear.

7 Store for six months then bottle and keep for another three months.

Note : This wine matures quite quickly.

WHITE WINES (*dry*)

APPLE WINE
Ingredients
10–12 lb windfall apples of mixed varieties including if possible some crab apples and, not more than half, eating apples
6 oz white grape juice concentrate per gallon
1–2 lb sugar
Water to 1 gallon
Pectolase
Campden tablets
$\frac{1}{2}$ teaspoonful citric acid
$\frac{1}{4}$ teaspoonful grape tannin
Burgundy yeast and nutrient

Method
1 Wash and crush the apples and drop them into just sufficient water to cover them, in which 1 teaspoonful Pectolase, $\frac{1}{2}$ level teaspoonful citric acid and 1 crushed Campden tablet has already been dissolved.

2 Two days later stir in the grape juice concentrate and check the specific gravity.

3 Stir in the tannin, nutrient and active yeast and ferment on the pulp for 7 days.

4 Strain out and press the solids, check the specific gravity and stir in sufficient sugar and water to make the quantity up to 1 gallon and the specific gravity to 1.085.

5 Fit an air lock and ferment to dryness.

6 Rack into a clean jar and as soon as the wine is clear, rack again, add a crushed Campden tablet and store for six months.

7 Bottle and store for a further six months.

APRICOT WINE

Ingredients

15 oz can of apricot pulp
6 oz white grape juice concentrate
2 lb sugar
Water to 1 gallon
1 teaspoonful citric acid
¼ teaspoonful grape tannin
1 teaspoonful Pectolase
Campden tablet
Hock yeast and nutrient

Method

1 Put the apricot pulp and syrup in a saucepan together with two cans of water. Bring to the boil and simmer till the fruit is soft.

2 Pour the must into a mashing vessel and when cool stir in the citric acid, tannin and Pectolase.

3 Cover the vessel and leave it in a warm place for 2 days.

4 Stir in the grape juice concentrate, 1 lb sugar, the yeast and nutrient and ferment on the pulp for 3 days.

5 Strain out the solids and press gently.

6 Stir in the remaining sugar, top up to 1 gallon with cold boiled water, fit an air lock and continue fermentation to dryness.

7 Rack into a clean jar and add 1 crushed Campden tablet.

8 Rack again when clear, store for four months then bottle and keep for a further four to six months.

PEACH WINE

Ingredients

15 oz can peach pulp (not halves or slices)
6 oz white grape juice concentrate
2 lb sugar
2 teaspoonfuls citric acid
¼ teaspoonful grape tannin
Burgundy yeast and nutrient
1 teaspoonful Pectolase
Water to 1 gallon
Campden tablets

Method

Exactly as for apricot wine.

FOLLY WINE
Ingredients
This wine is made from the non-fruiting shoots and thinning of grape vines. The name comes from the French word 'feuille' meaning leaves.
2 gallons of leaves, tendrils and thinnings
6 oz white grape juice concentrate
2 lb sugar
Water to 1 gallon
Pectolase
Campden tablets
Hock yeast and nutrient

Method
1 Wash the folly and shake off the surplus water.
2 Cut the tendrils into 3 in. lengths and place them in a saucepan.
3 Pour on 2 quarts water and bring to the boil.
4 Simmer gently till tender (20–30 minutes) turning the folly over from time to time.
5 Pour the must into a mashing vessel and when cool stir in 1 teaspoonful Pectolase and 1 Campden tablet.
6 Stir twice daily for 3–4 days then strain out the solids and press the folly dry.
7 Stir in the grape juice concentrate, the sugar, nutrient and an active yeast. Top up the jar to 1 gallon with cold boiled water, fit an air lock and ferment to dryness.
8 Rack into a clean jar, add 1 crushed Campden tablet and store for six months, then bottle and keep for a further six months.
Note: This is a surprisingly pleasant wine when well made and mature.

GOOSEBERRY WINE
Ingredients
3 lb gooseberries
6 oz white grape juice concentrate
2¼ lb sugar
Water to 1 gallon
Campden tablets
¼ teaspoonful grape tannin
Pectolase
Burgundy yeast and nutrient

Method

1 Wash, top and tail the gooseberries which should be green and firm.

2 Pour on 6 pints boiling water and when cool mash the berries with your hands.

3 Stir in 1 teaspoonful Pectolase and 1 Campden tablet, cover and leave for twenty-four hours.

4 Stir in the grape juice concentrate, the tannin, nutrient and the yeast and ferment on the pulp for 3 days stirring twice daily.

5 Strain out the solids and press, then stir in the sugar.

6 Fit an air lock and continue fermentation to dryness.

7 Siphon into a clean jar, add 1 crushed Campden tablet and store for six months, then bottle and keep for at least six months and preferably longer. This wine improves with three or four years storage.

GREENGAGE WINE

Ingredients

3 lb firm greengages
6 oz white grape juice concentrate
2¼ lb sugar
1 teaspoonful Pectolase
½ teaspoonful grape tannin
Campden tablets
Water to 1 gallon
Burgundy yeast and nutrient

Method

1 Wash and stalk the greengages and pour on 3 quarts boiling water.

2 When cool mash the fruit and remove the stones.

3 Stir in the Pectolase, 1 crushed Campden tablet and the tannin. Cover and leave for twenty-four hours.

4 Stir in the grape juice concentrate, the nutrient and an active yeast. Ferment on the pulp for 4 days stirring twice daily.

5 Strain out the solids and press gently.

6 Stir in the sugar, fit an air lock and ferment to dryness.

7 Rack into a clean jar add 1 crushed Campden tablet, store for six months then bottle and keep for a further six or nine months.

RHUBARB WINE

Ingredients

4–5 lb fresh rhubarb gathered in May or June
6 oz white grape juice concentrate
2¼ lb sugar
¼ teaspoonful grape tannin
Water to 1 gallon
Pectolase
Campden tablets
The rind only of 1 large lemon
Burgundy yeast and nutrient

Method

1 Cut off the leaves and 1 in. of stem together with the white root ends of enough stalks to leave a finished weight of 4 lb fruit.
2 Wash the stalks and wipe them clean, then chop them into 1 in. lengths about ½ in. in diameter.
3 Place them in a mashing vessel together with the lemon rind, pour on 3 quarts boiling water. When cool stir in 1 teaspoonful Pectolase and 1 crushed Campden tablet. Cover the vessel and leave for twenty-four hours.
4 Stir in the grape juice concentrate, the nutrient, tannin and an active yeast and ferment on the pulp for 4–5 days stirring twice daily.
5 Strain out the solids and press the pulp dry. Stir in the sugar fit an air lock and ferment to dryness.
6 Siphon into a clean jar add 1 crushed Campden tablet and store for as long as you can : twelve months or so. Bottle and keep for another six months.
Since this wine has a higher than usual acid content it will keep well.

WHITE WINES (*sweet*)

ELDERFLOWER WINE

Ingredients

1 pint elderflower florets, picked from their stalk and pressed down
12 oz white grape juice concentrate
2¼ lb sugar
½ oz citric acid
¼ teaspoonful grape tannin
Water to 1 gallon

Campden tablets
Sauterne yeast (no nutrient)

Method

1 Place the florets – excluding all green stems in a vessel and pour on 2 quarts hot water at about 150°F.
2 Stir in the acid and tannin and when cool 1 Campden tablet.
3 Macerate the florets with a wooden spoon several times a day for 3 days keeping the vessel closely covered meanwhile.
4 Strain the liquor on to the grape juice concentrate and sugar. Top up with water to 1 gallon and check that the specific gravity is between 1.095 and 1.100. Adjust if necessary.
5 Stir in the active yeast, fit an air lock and ferment to specific gravity 1.015.
6 Proceed with racking and crushed Campden tablets as indicated for Rosehip wine.

GRAPE JUICE CONCENTRATE WINE
Ingredients
27 fl oz white grape juice concentrate
1¼ lb white sugar
2 teaspoonfuls citric acid
½ teaspoonful grape tannin
Water to 1 gallon
Campden tablets
Sauterne yeast (no nutrient)

Method
1 Dissolve the grape juice concentrate, sugar, acid and tannin in 6 pints hot water. Top up to 1 gallon and when cool check that the specific gravity is between 1.095 and 1.100.
2 Stir in an active yeast and ferment in a warm place till the specific gravity reaches 1.015.
3 Proceed with racking and crushed Campden tablets as indicated for Rosehip wine.

RAISIN WINE
Ingredients
5 lb large raisins
1–1½ lb demerara sugar
½ teaspoonful grape tannin

1 teaspoonful Pectolase
Campden tablets
2 teaspoonfuls citric acid
Water to 1 gallon
Sauterne yeast (no nutrient)

Method

1 Chop the raisins being careful not to break the pips.
2 Pour 6 pints boiling water on to them.
3 When cool stir in the citric acid, tannin, Pectolase and 1 crushed Campden tablet. Cover and leave for 2 days, stirring twice daily.
4 Proceed as for Sultana wine.

ROSEHIP WINE

Ingredients

12 oz bottle rosehip syrup
6 oz white grape juice concentrate
2¼ lb sugar
½ oz citric acid
¼ teaspoonful grape tannin
Campden tablets
Water to 1 gallon
Sauterne yeast (no nutrient)

Method

1 Boil the sugar and citric acid in 4 pints water for 20 minutes.
2 When cool stir in the rosehip syrup, grape juice concentrate and active yeast and top up to 1 gallon.
3 Check the specific gravity which should be between 1.095 and 1.100.
4 Fit an air lock and ferment in a warm place.
5 Check the specific gravity from time to time and when it reaches 1.015 add two crushed Campden tablets and move the jar to a cold position.
6 As soon as the wine begins to clear, usually within a few days, rack it into a clean jar, refitting the air lock for safety.
7 Rack again a few days later when a further sediment appears and again as soon as the wine is bright, adding another Campden tablet before storing the wine for six months prior to bottling.
Note : The frequent racking will remove yeast cells and the addition of crushed Campden tablets will inhibit yeast growth. The wine will stabilise fairly sweet.

SULTANA WINE
Ingredients
5 lb chopped or minced sultanas
1 lb bananas
1½–2 lb sugar
Rinds and juice of 2 medium sized lemons
¼ teaspoonful grape tannin
Water to 1 gallon
Pectolase
Campden tablets
Sauterne yeast (no nutrient).

Method
1 Wash and chop or mince the sultanas, peel and mash the bananas, wash and thinly pare the lemons.
2 Put these ingredients in a vessel and pour on 6 pints hot water at about 150°F.
3 When cool stir in 1 teaspoonful Pectolase and 1 crushed Campden tablet, cover and leave for forty-eight hours, stirring twice daily.
4 Take out sufficient liquor to check the specific gravity and stir in the active yeast.
5 Ferment on the pulp for 4 days then strain and press the pulp.
6 Stir in sufficient sugar and water to make a specific gravity between 1.095 and 1.100 in a gallon of must.
7 Fit an air lock and ferment at 70°F. to specific gravity 1.015.
8 Proceed with racking and crushed Campden tablets as indicated for Rosehip wine.

III GRAPE WINES – RED, ROSÉ AND WHITE

Many people now grow a few vines in their garden especially in the South of England. Several excellent wines can be made from them. In general they are somewhat acid through insufficient sunshine and so need dilution with water and the addition of sugar. Imported grapes may be used, but these are usually dessert varieties light in acid. Perhaps the best of these are the seedless grapes imported from Cyprus in July and August. Always use the best grapes you can get. Any that are loose or in less than perfect condition should be thoroughly washed in water containing 2 or 3 crushed Campden tablets and ½ oz citric acid, rinsed in clean cold water and shaken fairly dry before they are crushed.

ENGLISH BLACK GRAPES
Method
1 Weigh your crop. Remove the main stalks and crush the berries without breaking the pips.
2 Squeeze out the juice. From 20 lb grapes you will express about 1 gallon.
3 Check the gravity, pour the juice into a fermentation jar, add an active Pommard yeast, fit an air lock and leave in the warm to ferment.
4 Pour ½ gallon of tepid water over the pulp and macerate it thoroughly with freshly washed hands, that have been thoroughly rinsed from the smell of soap. Strain off some of the must and check the specific gravity.
5 Add some active yeast, 1 teaspoonful of citric acid, ½ teaspoonful of tannin and 1 nutrient tablet. Stir thoroughly and cover closely.
6 Stir well twice daily for 6 days, then strain and press the pulp.
7 Add the two specific gravity readings together, divide by 3 and multiply by 2 so that you know the specific gravity per gallon. Mix the two musts together.
8 Add sufficient sugar to raise this figure to 1.080 and continue fermentation to dryness.

ENGLISH WHITE GRAPES
Method
1 Proceed as for black grapes but only ferment on the pulp for 2 days. Use a Hock yeast for preference. 1 lb only of light honey may be used instead of ¾ lb sugar.
2 Mature this wine for twelve months before serving chilled.

ROSÉ
Ingredients
If you haven't sufficient black grapes to make a gallon of wine, add them to an apple wine to produce a light rosé
40 lb mixed apples, cooking, dessert and if possible some crab apples
5–15 lb English black grapes
10 lb sugar

H

Champagne yeast
1 heaped teaspoonful grape tannin
1 oz-citric acid
2 nutrient tablets
Campden tablets
3 gallons cold water

Method

1 Wash the apples, remove any bad portions, crush them and drop them into a vessel containing 2 gallons of cold water in which the citric acid and 2 Campden tablets have been dissolved.

2 Wash the grapes, remove the main stalks, crush the berries and add to the apple must.

3 Pour on sufficient water just to cover the fruit and lay a large plate on the surface to keep the pulp just submerged. This prevents the apple from browning (oxidation) and imparting an off-flavour to the wine.

4 Next day stir in an active Champagne yeast, the nutrient and the tannin.

5 As soon as fermentation starts, press the juice from some pulp and check the specific gravity.

6 Ferment on the pulp for 7 days, then strain and press the pulp dry.

7 Stir in from 6–10 lb sugar – sufficient to raise the specific gravity to 1.080 when the total volume of the must is increased to 5 gallons. The apples and the grapes will produce a considerable quantity of juice and sugar and very little if any extra water may be needed.

8 Continue fermentation under an air lock till the wine is dry then rack, store and bottle as usual. This makes a delicious dry rosé that is excellent served chilled on a hot summer's day.

Note : White grapes may be used instead of black and the wine will then of course, be white instead of rosé.

CYPRIOT SEEDLESS GRAPES

Ingredients
18–20 lb grapes
2 quarts water
2 teaspoonfuls citric acid
½ teaspoonful grape tannin
Hock yeast

1½–2 lb sugar
Campden tablets

Method

1 Pick over and wash the grapes in a sulphite solution.

2 Crush the berries, strain off the juice and check the specific gravity. Pour the juice into a fermentation jar, stir in an active Hock yeast and fit an air lock.

3 Pour 2 quarts cold water over the grape pulp. Stir in the citric acid, grape tannin and 1 crushed Campden tablet. Cover and leave for twenty-four hours.

4 Strain and press the pulp dry. Check the specific gravity. Mix the two musts together. Add the two specific gravities together multiply 3, divide by 2 and add sufficient sugar to raise the figure to 1.080 (1 lb sugar=about 32 units).

5 Ferment to dryness, rack and add 1 crushed Campden tablet per gallon. Store for two months, rack, repeat the Campden tablet, store for four months then bottle.

6 When the wine is a year old, serve it chilled with light food.

IV SPARKLING WINES – RED, ROSÉ AND WHITE

The sparkle is caused by carbon dioxide gas formed during bottle fermentation when the wine is laid down to mature. It is important that the wine should be star bright before it is bottled and that no pulp residue remains. Only unchipped, unscratched Champagne bottles should be used, since the pressure that builds up during bottle fermentation would burst all ordinary wine bottles as well as imperfect Champagne bottles. Plastic or cork stoppers may be used, provided they give a good air tight fit. They must be wired on to the bottle to prevent them being blown out by the pressure of the gas.

Since a secondary fermentation is essential, the initial specific gravity should not exceed 1.080 so that the volume of alcohol in the finished wine does not exceed 10 per cent. If the wine is too strong the yeast may not be able to ferment the added sugar. This would result in a sweetened still wine.

Bottles should be stored on their side after the secondary fermentation and a distinctive feathery shaped deposit will be thrown. Before serving this can be worked down on to the cork by upending the bottle and giving it a little twist every day for a week or so. When the deposit is firmly on the cork. Freeze the neck of the bottle in crushed ice containing an equal quantity of salt. This takes 30–45 minutes. Carefully remove the cork and frozen sediment whilst holding the bottle upside down, then quickly slide your thumb over the neck, gently restore the bottle to the vertical. Insert a new cork already placed close at hand. Serve within a few days at a temperature of 45–50°F. This may be achieved by leaving the bottle in a refrigerator for one hour.

Alternatively the bottle may be stood upright for a few days for the sediment to collect in the punt, great care must be taken when pouring the wine to ensure that the sediment is not disturbed.

SPARKLING APPLE WINE
Ingredients
6–8 lb best quality apples of mixed varieties if possible. Preferably in the proportions of two-thirds cooking apples to one-third eating apples. It is important not to use bruised or damaged apples
½ pint white grape juice concentrate
1–1½ lb white sugar
3 quarts of cold water
1 teaspoonful citric acid
⅛ teaspoonful tannin
1 teaspoonful Pectolase
Champagne yeast
Nutrient
Campden tablet

Method
1 Pour the water into a mashing vessel and dissolve 1 crushed Campden tablet, 1 teaspoonful citric acid and 1 teaspoonful Pectolase in it.
2 Wash the apples, crush them thoroughly a few at a time and drop them quickly into the water.
3 Lay a large plate on top of the floating fruit to keep it beneath the surface of the water and so prevent oxidation, or browning as it is called. Cover the vessel and leave it overnight.
4 Next day stir in the grape juice concentrate and when it is thoroughly dissolved strain out enough must to fill an hydrometer jar. Check the specific gravity and record the reading.

5 Add an active Champagne yeast, nutrient and tannin and ferment on the pulp for 7 days.

6 Strain and press the pulp. Check the specific gravity of the must. Stir in sufficient sugar to increase the specific gravity from the recorded readings to 1.080 – no higher.

7 Ferment under an air lock to dryness.

8 When the wine begins to clear, rack into a clean jar. Repeat the process as deposits fall until the wine is star bright.

9 Bottle into sterile Champagne bottles.

10 Make up a sugar syrup of ¼ pint water and 8 oz white sugar thoroughly dissolved and clear. Add 1 dessert spoonful (½ oz) to each bottle of wine.

11 Also add to each bottle 1 teaspoonful of an active Champagne yeast, previously prepared.

12 Cork tightly and wire down the corks. Label the bottles with date of making and date of bottling with the added sugar and yeast.

13 Stand the bottles in a warm place for two weeks and then move them to a cool store for one year.

14 Before serving either remove the deposit as indicated or stand the bottles upright for several days.

15 Serve the wine chilled on a festive occasion with food of your choice.

SPARKLING PEAR WINE

Ingredients
6 lb hand picked cooking pears
1–1½ lb white sugar
½ pint white grape juice concentrate
3 quarts of cold water
1 teaspoonful citric acid
1 teaspoonful Pectolase
Champagne yeast
Nutrient
Campden tablet

Method
1 Pour the water into a mashing vessel and dissolve 1 crushed Campden tablet, 1 teaspoonful citric acid and 1 teaspoonful Pectolase in it.

2 Wash the pears, crush them thoroughly a few at a time and drop them quickly into the water.

3 Lay a large plate on top of the floating fruit to keep it beneath the surface of water and so prevent oxidation. Cover the vessel and leave it overnight.

4 Next day stir in the grape juice concentrate and when it is thoroughly dissolved strain out enough must to fill an hydrometer jar. Check the specific gravity and record the reading.

5 Add an active Champagne yeast and a nutrient and ferment on the pulp for 7 days.

6 Strain and press the pulp. Check the specific gravity of the must. Stir in sufficient sugar to increase the specific gravity from the recorded readings to 1.080 – no higher.

7 Ferment under an air lock to dryness.

8 When the wine begins to clear, rack into a clean jar. Repeat the process as deposits fall until the wine is star bright.

9 Bottle into sterile Champagne bottles.

10 Make up a sugar syrup of $\frac{1}{4}$ pint water and 8 oz white sugar thoroughly dissolved and clear. Add 1 dessert spoonful ($\frac{1}{2}$ oz) to each bottle of wine.

11 Also add to each bottle 1 teaspoonful of an active Champagne yeast, previously prepared.

12 Cork tightly and wire down the corks. Label the bottles with date of making and date of bottling with the added sugar and yeast.

13 Stand the bottles in a warm place for two weeks and then move them to a cool store for one year.

14 Before serving either remove the deposit as indicated or stand the bottles upright for several days.

15 Serve the wine chilled on a festive occasion with food of your choice.

SPARKLING GOOSEBERRY WINE

Ingredients

2 lb green gooseberries
$\frac{1}{2}$ pint white grape juice concentrate
$1\frac{1}{2}$ lb white sugar
3 quarts hot water
Campden tablet
Pectolase

Nutrient
Champagne yeast

Method

1 Wash, top and tail the gooseberries, place them in a mashing vessel and pour boiling water on them.

2 When cool crush the now softened fruit pulp with your hands, add one crushed Campden tablet, 1 teaspoonful of Pectolase, cover and leave for forty-eight hours.

3 Stir in the grape juice concentrate, and then proceed as already indicated, in the two previous recipes.

SPARKLING ROSÉ WINE

Ingredients

3 lb redcurrants
4 oz black grape juice concentrate
1½ lb sugar
Champagne yeast
Nutrient
Pectolase
Campden tablet
3 quarts water

Method

1 Wash and crush the currants and pour cold water over them.

2 Stir in 1 teaspoonful Pectolase and 1 crushed Campden tablet.

3 Cover and leave for twenty-four hours.

4 Stir in the grape juice concentrate and check the specific gravity. Stir in the nutrient and active yeast, cover and place in a warm position for 4 days.

5 Strain out the solids, check the specific gravity again and stir in sufficient sugar to make the total specific gravity up to 1.080.

6 Continue as for sparkling apple wine.

SPARKLING RED WINE

Ingredients

2 lb apples
1 lb best quality fresh elderberries
½ pint black grape juice concentrate
1½ lb white sugar
3 quarts water
1 teaspoonful citric acid

Champagne yeast
Campden tablet
Pectolase
Nutrient

Method
1 Pick all stalks off the elderberries and rinse them clean.
2 Place them in a saucepan with 1 quart water and gently bring
them to the boil. Remove from heat and leave them to cool.
3 Prepare the apples as for sparkling apple wine and add the
elderberries and grape juice concentrate.
4 Continue as set out in the previous recipes.

V DESSERT WINES – RED, ROSÉ AND WHITE

To be enjoyed to perfection a dessert wine needs to be of pleasing
flavour, full bodied, sweet, strong and with an appropriate balance
of acid and tannin. It is meant to be served at the end of or just
after a meal. Having enjoyed other wines with different courses
in the meal it follows that the dessert wine should be of high
quality and character. The earlier wines should lead up to the
dessert wine.

The recipes that follow have all produced superb wines, but
they do need a longer period of maturation than tables wines. Two
years is a minimum and most of these wines may not be at their
best for 3–5 years and will keep for many more. This is the
price of quality and it is well worth paying for these selected
wines. They should all be served free from chill at about 67°F.

BLACK BEAUTY
Ingredients
5 lb fresh ripe blackberries
2 lb windfall apples
½ pint black grape juice concentrate
1 lb bananas
1 teaspoonful Pectolase
3 lb sugar
7 pints water
1 teaspoonful citric acid
Port yeast
Nutrient
Campden tablets

Method

1 Crush the Campden tablet and dissolve it with the citric acid in 7 pints cold water in a mashing vessel.

2 Stalk and wash the blackberries, shake them free of surplus water, crush them with a wooden spoon and add them to the water.

3 Wash and crush the apples and add them to the vessel.

4 Peel the bananas, mash them with a fork and add them to the rest of the fruit.

5 Sprinkle on the Pectolase, stir the mash well, cover it closely and leave it to stand for twenty-four hours.

6 Stir in the grape juice concentrate and when it is thoroughly dissolved check the specific gravity with an hydrometer. Make a note of the reading.

7 Stir in the nutrient and active Port yeast and ferment on the pulp for 7 days.

8 Strain out the solids and squeeze them dry.

9 Stir in 2 lb sugar and continue the fermentation under an air lock and in a warm position.

10 One week later stir in another ½ lb sugar, replace the air lock and continue the fermentation.

11 As fermentation slows down check the specific gravity and when it reaches 1.010 or less stir in the remaining ½ lb sugar.

12 At specific gravity 1.016 rack the wine into a clean vessel and add a crushed Campden tablet.

13 Rack again as soon as a deposit appears.

14 When there is no further fermentation, rack again, bung tight, label and store for eighteen months. Check occasionally and if needs be rack the wine off any deposit that may form.

15 Bottle and store for at least six months before serving free from chill.

This is an excellent wine served with blue stilton cheese, a Cox's apple and dry biscuits.

DAMSON DELIGHT

Ingredients
3 lb black ripe damsons
1 lb apples – any variety
½ pint black grape juice concentrate
3 lb sugar

I

7 pints water
Port yeast and nutrient
1 teaspoonful citric acid
¼ teaspoonful grape tannin
1 teaspoonful Pectolase
1 Campden tablet

Method

1 Wash and stalk the damsons and wash and crush the apples.
2 Pour the boiling water over them, add the citric acid and leave to cool.
3 Crush the damsons with your hands and remove the stones.
4 Stir in the grape juice concentrate, the Pectolase, tannin, nutrient and active yeast.
5 Cover the vessel and place it in a warm position.
6 Ferment on the pulp for seven days then strain out the solids and stir in 1 lb sugar.
7 Fit an air lock and continue fermentation.
8 One week later stir in another 1 lb sugar and repeat the process with the final 1 lb sugar the following week.
9 Leave the fermenting must in a warm place until fermentation is finished, then remove it to a cool place so that the wine can clear.
10 Rack the new wine from its sediment, add a crushed Campden tablet and store for two months.
11 Rack again and store for one year then bottle and keep for at least six months.
12 Serve this wine free from chill with English cheese.

ELDERBERRY THE GREAT

Ingredients
3 lb best black ripe elderberries
½ lb dried bilberries or 15 oz can of bilberries
¼ pint black grape juice concentrate
1 lb apples any variety
1 lb peeled ripe bananas
3¼ lb sugar
1 gallon water
Rind and juice of 2 lemons
Port yeast and nutrient

1 teaspoonful Pectolase
1 Campden tablet

Method

1 Pour 1 gallon of cold water into a mashing vessel and stir in the lemon juice, Pectolase and crushed Campden tablet.
2 Wash and crush the apples and place in the water at once.
3 Stalk, wash and crush the elderberries and add to the apples.
4 Peel and mash the bananas and add to the must.
5 Wash the dried bilberries and add to the must or pour in the contents of the can.
6 Cover closely and leave for twenty-four hours.
7 Next day stir in the grape juice concentrate, the nutrient and an active yeast.
8 Ferment on the pulp for 7 days in a warm place.
9 Strain out the solids and stir in 1 lb sugar.
10 Fit an air lock and continue fermentation adding the remaining sugar in two 1 lb doses at weekly intervals as indicated for Damson Delight and other wines.
11 Rack and store as similarly indicated mature for two years.

This is a rich and famous wine well worth the making – but don't drink too much!

KENTISH CREAM

Ingredients

2 lb black Morello cherries
3 pints strong ale or star bright home-brewed beer, not too 'hoppy'
1½ lb demerara sugar dissolved in ½ pint warm water.
Juice only 1 large lemon
Madeira yeast and nutrient

Method

1 Wash and stalk the cherries, split them and remove the stones.
2 Place them in a suitable vessel, gently pour on the beer and gently stir in the sugar syrup.
3 Equally gently stir in the lemon juice, nutrient and active yeast.
4 Cover the vessel with polythene secured by an elastic band and place it in a warm position.
5 Ferment on the pulp for 7 days then strain out the solids, pressing gently.

6 Continue fermentation under an air lock until fermentation ceases and the wine begins to clear.

7 Rack from the sediment into a clean jar and store for two months then rack again.

8 When the wine is quite clear it may be bottled into 13 oz, or similar, bottles, corked and labelled and stored for one year.

Note : This wine has the bouquet and flavour of cherry brandy and should be appreciated with great respect.

DAMSON CREAM
Instead of Morello cherries, damsons may be used in the above recipe. They should be of superb quality, large, ripe, black and rich. It is a waste to use poor quality fruit.

NAPOLEON
Ingredients
2 lb old potatoes
2 lb chopped raisins
1 lb crushed, flaked or malted wheat
1 large cooking apple
Rind and juice of 2 large lemons
Rind and juice of 1 large orange
3 lb demerara sugar
1 teaspoonful Pectolase
Campden tablet
Tokay yeast and nutrient tablet
1 gallon water

Method
1 Scrub the potatoes absolutely clean and chop them into small pieces. Wash the wheat. Thinly pare the orange and lemons. Wash the raisins and chop them. Wash and crush the apple last of all.

2 Put all these ingredients into a mashing vessel, pour a gallon of boiling water over them and cover the vessel.

3 When the must is cool stir in the expressed juice of the orange and lemons, the Pectolase, nutrient and active yeast.

4 Cover the vessel and ferment on the pulp for 5 days.

5 Strain out the solids, stir in 1 lb sugar, fit an air lock and place in a warm position.

6 One week later remove some wine, dissolve 1 lb sugar in it, return it to the fermentation jar and refix the air lock.

7 One week later repeat the procedure and continue fermentation until it stops.

8 Remove the jar to a cool place and as soon as the wine begins to clear, rack into a clean jar and add a crushed Campden tablet.

9 Rack again a month later, then store for one year at least.

10 Bottle and keep for two years.

Note : This is a very strong dessert wine of great character if properly matured for at least three years.

PEACH PARFAIT

Ingredients

4 lb fresh peaches
Rind and juice of 1 large lemon
½ pint white grape juice concentrate
2½–3 lb white sugar
4–6 pints water
Sauterne yeast and nutrient
Pectolase
Campden tablets

Method

1 Select ripe peaches that are still firm and free from any blemished portions, Split them so that you can remove and discard the stones, then cut the peaches into small pieces.

2 Pour on 4 pints cold water and stir in 1 crushed Campden tablet, the rind and juice of the lemon and 2 teaspoonfuls of Pectolase. Cover the vessel closely and leave it in a warm position for twenty-four hours.

3 Next day stir in the white grape juice concentrate dissolved in half a pint of warm water, the nutrient and an active yeast.

4 Re-cover the vessel and ferment on the pulp for 5 days only.

5 Strain out the solids, pressing but gently. If needs be add sufficient cold water to bring the total quantity of must up to 8 pints. Subsequent additions of sugar will increase the quantity and this will be useful in topping up after racking off the sediment.

6 Stir in 1½ lb sugar and continue fermentation at a temperature of 70°F. under an air lock.

7 One week later remove some wine, dissolve 1 lb sugar in it, return it to the jar and continue fermentation.

8 When fermentation begins to slow down check the specific gravity and when 1.010 is reached stir in another ½ lb sugar.

9 When fermentation ceases and the wine begins to clear, check the specific gravity which should be not less than 1.010 and if needs be add a little more sugar. Rack the wine into a clean jar.

10 Add 1 crushed Campden tablet and store the wine for 4 weeks, well corked and labelled.

11 As a further deposit forms, rack again.

12 When the wine is clear add another crushed Campden tablet and store for a year, then bottle and keep for another year if possible.

SLOE SERENE

Ingredients

3 lb ripe sloes
1 lb cooking apples
1 lb bananas
2 large lemons
½ pint grape juice concentrate
½ teaspoonful tannin
3 lb sugar
7 pints water
1 teaspoonful Pectolase
Port yeast and nutrient

Method

1 Stalk and wash the sloes; place them in a mashing vessel and pour boiling water on them.

2 Peel and mash the bananas and add to the sloes.

3 Wash and crush the apples and add to the sloes.

4 Thinly pare the lemons and add the peel to the sloes.

5 Stir in the grape juice concentrate and Pectolase.

6 Cover the vessel and allow the must to cool to 70°F.

7 Cut the lemons in half and squeeze out the juice – stir into the must together with the nutrient, tannin and active port yeast.

8 Cover the vessel again and leave the must to ferment on the pulp for 6–7 days.

9 Strain and press the pulp, stir in 1 lb sugar and continue fermentation under an air lock.

10 One week later stir in another 1 lb sugar and one week later still stir in the final 1 lb sugar.

11 When fermentation is finished rack and store for one month

then rack again and as frequently as necessary till the wine is bright.

12 Store for one year at least then bottle and keep for another year if possible.

Note : This is a strong dessert wine of good body and flavour.

Index

Recipes are set in *italic*